The
AC Electrics

The
AC Electrics

Colin J. Marsden

An imprint of
Ian Allan Publishing

Contents

Below: *Restored by Alstom Willesden into as near as possible original 'electric blue', Class 86 No 86233 became the flagship of the fleet following repaint in 2002. Named* Vulcan Heritage, *it is seen approaching Birmingham International station on 23 July 2003 leading the 08.40 Euston-Wolverhampton service. This locomotive is owned by HSBC Rail and stored at Oxley.* **Author**

First published 2007

ISBN (10) 0 86093 614 7
ISBN (13) 978 0 86093 614 5

Published by Oxford Publishing Co

an imprint of Ian Allan Publishing Ltd, Hersham, Surrey KT12 4RG.
Printed in England by Ian Allan Printing Ltd, Hersham, Surrey KT12 4RG.

Code: 0709/B

Visit the Ian Allan Publishing website at www.ianallanpublishing.com

Introduction

Welcome to *The AC Electrics*. When looking at the vast list of railway books published, it seems that over the years since the introduction of what we all call 'modern traction', very few titles have been produced dedicated entirely to the electric classes, when viewed in context to the number of books published on diesel traction. This is likely to be due to the greater interest in diesel classes and the original domination of diesel traction as a replacement for steam in the middle years of the 20th century.

Today, the vast majority of new trains are powered by electricity and this is demonstrated by the sizeable number of classes introduced in recent years, mainly of the electric multiple-unit (EMU) type. However, a sizeable fleet of electric locomotives is still in service operating front-line passenger and freight duties.

Alternating current (AC) electric power, although considered a recent development, was pioneered in the UK in 1908 on the Lancaster-Morecambe-Heysham line as an experiment in the use of electric propulsion in a rail environment. Over the ensuing years AC power, although introduced on some South London routes, was overtaken by the development of direct current (DC) traction systems and it was not until the 1950s that AC power returned as the preferred choice for future electrification systems.

As by this time such a large part of the Southern Region of the BTC was using DC power collected from the third rail, this method of propulsion was retained in the area, but all other parts of the UK, with the exception of the Liverpool suburban area, opted for overhead AC power systems, using the industrial voltage and frequency of 25,000V AC at 50 cycles.

The principal user of electric main line traction was the BTC/BR London Midland Region on the West Coast routes, which were electrified in the 1960s and gradually extended to include London-Scotland from the early 1970s. On this route a number of high-output lightweight electric classes have been used and it is only in the very recent past that these have given way to modern state-of-the-art electric unit train formations.

This title covers in words and illustrations all the AC types that have operated on the UK rail network under the BTC, BR and now privatised railway network. The dual-voltage AC/DC EMUs have also been included for completeness.

Although many other electric railway operators throughout the world are still developing AC electric locomotives, it is unlikely that any further development or introduction of such types will be made in the UK, the last major class being the Class 92s designed and built for use on Anglo-Europe Channel Tunnel freight services. It is likely in the future that new passenger trains will follow the electric unit style and when our present fleets of electric locomotives are phased out from freight flows their replacements are more likely to be diesel. The only real chance of furthering the use of AC technology in the UK is to have a mainland European builder offer a product built to the restricted UK loading gauge.

I would like to record my thanks to the many people who have assisted with information and illustrations for inclusion in this book.

Colin J. Marsden
Dawlish
August 2007

Below: *One of the most successful of the modern AC electric multiple-unit train sets has been the Class 321, presently working for 'one' Great Eastern, Silverlink and Northern. On 12 July 2006, set No 321438 departs from Stratford with an Ipswich to Liverpool Street semi-fast service. The livery carried is based on the First Great Eastern colours.* **Author's collection**

The early AC years

The use of alternating current (AC) power in the UK rail traction industry has really only been around in any great scale for about 50 years. However, one or two earlier applications must be recorded.

One of the most interesting early developments was a Metropolitan Vickers (MV) contract placed by the Midland Railway in 1906 for the electrification of the 9.5-mile line between Lancaster, Morecambe and the port of Heysham which opened between Morecambe and Heysham in April 1908, using 6,600V AC single phase power supply at 25 cycles; the route was extended to Lancaster Green Ayre and Castle stations later the same year.

This was very much a development project. Three motor coaches and several trailers with driving controls were built. Two power cars were originally fitted with bow power collectors and Siemens traction equipment, while the third had a pantograph and Westinghouse equipment. Trains of two- to four-car formation could be operated.

With world hostilities in the following years and finance needed in other areas, no further extension of the Midland system took place. When the power equipment became life-expired in the early 1950s, the route was 'de-electrified' and reverted to steam traction.

Soon after the cessation of electric operation, world interest in electrification was booming, especially in mainland Europe where the French were pioneering the use of industrial frequency electric systems for rail application. The nascent BTC realised that the already-wired Morecambe–Heysham route could act as an important testing base for such developments in the UK.

Power for the line remained at 6,600V AC but was now fed at 50 cycles. Most of the original overhead power system remained, but one or two test sections for a possible 'high-speed' electric railway were incorporated.

The original stock was by now life-expired and the BTC authorised the rebuilding of three stored Siemens three-car sets previously used on the 1914 Willesden–Earls Court electric network. Three sets were modified in 1953 and fitted with English Electric equipment and a fourth followed in 1957 fitted with Metropolitan-Vickers equipment.

Under the new system, the AC power was collected by an overhead pantograph and transformed and rectified to 750V DC for traction purposes.

Following re-electrification the route became a major testing site for

Below: *For the 1925-authorised extension of the LB&SCR AC electrification, a fleet of 21 Motor Vans, or 'Milk Vans' as they became known, were ordered from Metropolitan Carriage, Wagon & Finance Company of Birmingham. These vehicles were basically a locomotive, fitted with driving cabs at each end, a guard's van in the centre and had two power collection 'bows' on the roof. Although these vehicles could lead a train, it was common to find them in the middle of a train formation, with two passenger cars at either end. Vehicle No 10101, the first of the build, is illustrated when brand new.*
Author's collection

early UK overhead power equipment and formed the normal passenger service between Morecambe and Heysham until line closure under the Beeching axe in January 1966.

A far more impressive early AC railway development was with the London, Brighton and South Coast Railway (LB&SCR), which received authorisation to electrify part of its network in 1903. The system to be adopted was a 6,700V AC overhead pickup.

The first route to be 'electrified' was the South London line between Victoria and London Bridge. Services were provided by a fleet of eight three-car sets built by Metropolitan Amalgamated Carriage & Wagon, traction coming from two 115hp Winter Eichberg motors under each driving cab. The first passengers to enjoy the electric network were carried in December 1909. Just a year after the trains' introduction the LB&SCR announced that they were to be re-formed as 16 two-car sets, as this better matched passenger demand.

Such was the success of the South London scheme that the LB&SCR Board agreed to extend the electrified network, the next route being the line from London to Crystal Palace via Streatham Hill. Trains for this route comprised 30 two-car driving motor and driving trailer sets built by Metropolitan Amalgamated Carriage & Wagon, plus 30 driving trailer cars built by the LB&SCR at Lancing.

By 1913 further extensions were planned, but after the outbreak of World War I in 1914 most were shelved for the duration of hostilities.

In 1918 agreement was made to electrify the main line from London to Brighton and Eastbourne. However, as time revealed, only the sections as far as Coulsdon North and Wallington were finished and opened to passenger services in April 1925. Rolling stock for this extension was noteworthy, comprising 21 motor vans (usually known as 'Milk Vans'), 60 driving trailers and 20 intermediate trailers. The 21 motor vans were basically a locomotive with driving controls at each end and a guard's van in the middle. Trains were usually formed as a five-car set with a motor van in the middle, with a trailer and a driving trailer at each end. The motor vans were constructed by Metropolitan Carriage, Wagon & Finance Co of Birmingham.

By 1926 some form of classification was introduced with the South London stock becoming 'SL', the London–Crystal Palace stock 'CP' and the main line London–Coulsdon/Wallington as 'CW'.

With the Grouping of the railways in 1923, the Southern Board quickly decided to follow the mass electrification of its lines but to use the more traditional third-rail DC method of power collection. It was therefore agreed in August 1926 to abandon the AC system and convert the routes to third-rail power supply. The first route to close to AC operation was the London–Crystal Palace line in June 1928, followed by the other routes in September 1929.

As many of the passenger vehicles built for AC operation had many years of operational life left, most were rebuilt to DC operation, while the motor vans were rebuilt as brake vehicles.

Below: In pristine ex-works condition, LB&SCR Crystal Palace line extension Driving Motor Third No 3236 is viewed from the cab and bow collector end at the Metropolitan Amalgamated Carriage & Wagon works in Saltley, Birmingham. **Author's collection**

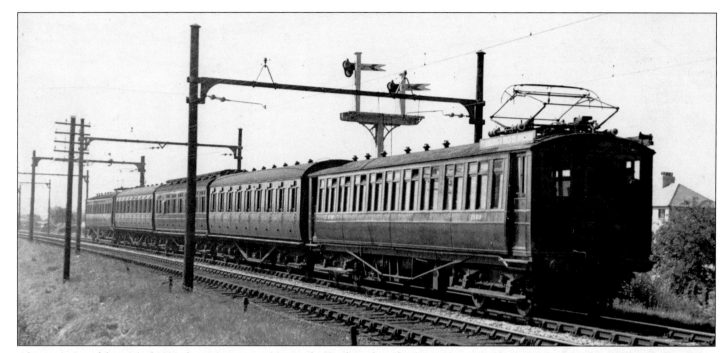

Above: *A view of the original 1908 alternating-current Morecambe-Heysham electrification stock, supplied to the Midland Railway. This view shows two single power cars either end of three loco-hauled trailers. This method of operation was carried out in the summer months when traffic levels were high. Although this was an AC overhead system, minutes of the period indicate that considerable research into the operation of electric traction in general was gathered from this project and developed into the first main-line UK electrification of the Woodhead route using overhead power collection, but in a DC format in the 1950s.* **W S Garth**

Above left and left: *Looking rather primitive when compared with more 'modern' electric multiple unit vehicles, Driving Motor No 28611 is seen complete with oil headlight near Heysham in the middle illustration and at Morecambe in the lower view, in the 1920s. It appears that it is not only today that we live in a 'nanny state' where everyone is advised and told of everything; note the warning board adjacent to the bow collector reading 'it is dangerous to touch this apparatus'. One wonders what the 'Motorman' of the era would make of some of today's highly sophisticated AC stock.* Both: **W Hubert Foster**

Above and below: *After becoming life-expired, the original 1908 Morecambe–Heysham electric units were withdrawn in the early 1950s. The chance was then seized to use the already electrified route to further development of AC power supply, but now using the industrial frequency of 50 cycles. To provide trains for the route, three and eventually four of the then stored 1914-built Willesden–Earls Court DC EMUs were rebuilt for AC operation. In the above view one of the 'new' sets is seen at Morecambe during very early pre-service trials. The view below is a very rare colour illustration of one of the sets, painted in BR standard multiple-unit green, complete with a red buffer beam.* **Author's collection**

Class 80

Design: Metropolitan-Vickers A1A-A1A 25kV overhead AC electric
Number range: E1000, renumbered E2001
Introduced: 1958
Withdrawn: 1968

Above: *Viewed from its non-pantograph or 'office' end, No E1000 is seen on training duties near Wilmslow. The locomotive is painted in BTC passenger black livery off-set by a silver body band. Note the trimmed buffers and original running light arrangement carried from when it was the gas turbine No 18100.* **Author's collection**

The first of the 25kV AC overhead power collection electric locomotive classes was a rather unusual locomotive. It was originally built as a gas-turbine locomotive in 1952 by Metropolitan-Vickers. Originally numbered 18100, it was operated by the BTC on the Western Region until made redundant in 1958.

Electrification of the West Coast main line between Euston, Birmingham and Manchester/Liverpool having been authorised, orders were placed for suitable traction. It was apparent that there would be a delay before any operational units would be available, and that staff training would be required since a totally new form of traction was being introduced. Steam drivers and maintenance staff were about to be launched into a new transport era.

Following much deliberation it was agreed by the BTC to contract Metropolitan-Vickers to rebuild its gas-turbine No 18100 into a 25kV AC overhead power collection electric locomotive. This would enable training as well as overhead power equipment to be tested prior to squadron delivery of production orders.

When authorised for conversion, No 18100 was parked out of use at Dukinfield near Manchester, from where it was hauled to the MV plant in Stockton-on-Tees. The rebuilding work was extensive and included removal of the gas turbine unit, auxiliary combustion equipment, direct-current power equipment, fuel tanks and control equipment. In their place alternating-current power, control, transformer and rectifier units were fitted. The driving cabs were also rebuilt to remove the Great Western Railway-style right-hand driving layout originally fitted.

The roof was also modified to accommodate a power collection pantograph. A structural modification worthy of note was the

trimming of the original buffers to bring the locomotive within the loading gauge of the LM route.

To provide traction power for the 'new' electric, four of the original six traction motors were retained, as were some of the auxiliary machines such as traction motor blowers, vacuum exhauster, air compressor and cooling equipment. During the rebuild work a small staff room or office was incorporated at No 1 end; this was intended as a training classroom and could seat five people.

The pioneer LM AC electric, finished in BTC main-line black livery offset by a silver body band, was released from Metropolitan-Vickers in autumn 1958, at the time still carrying its gas-turbine running number of 18100.

After initial tests in the Styal area the locomotive was renumbered as E1000 and put to work on the Manchester–Crewe line between Mauldeth Road and Wilmslow. After a short period No E1000 was renumbered as E2001.

After 12 months as the sole 25kV AC electric locomotive, the production classes started to enter traffic, spelling the end for No E2001. After mid-1961 it saw little use and in the autumn it was sent to Scotland and used on the Glasgow area electrified network for equipment testing, but by Christmas it was returned to the LMR, and stored at various locations such as Crewe, Goostrey and finally Rugby. For a period in 1964 No E2001 saw further use, as a training loco at Rugby, but after only a few months it was again stood down. By early 1968 it was deleted from stock, remaining for an extended period in sidings at Market Harborough and Rugby before being sold to J. Cashmore Ltd of Great Bridge for scrap in 1972.

Above: *In its original guise as a gas-turbine locomotive, No 18100 is seen on 4 March 1952 powering a Plymouth–Paddington test train towards Parsons Tunnel, Teignmouth. As a gas-turbine it developed 3,000hp and at the time of introduction was the most powerful locomotive in the UK.* **Author's collection**

Below: *Carrying its short-lived E1000 identity, the training electric is seen at Styal soon after delivery from the Metropolitan-Vickers factory in Stockton-on-Tees. The locomotive was fitted with one single-arm pantograph at its No 1 end. Note that the between-bogie area is empty of equipment.* **Author's collection**

Above: *Again viewed from its No 1 or pantograph end, No E1000 is seen with the pantograph in the lowered position. During the rebuilding work, a new roof section was provided which had roughly half its length as a low flat section. Although not identifiable from the picture, the rebuilding work also saw the centre wheelset of each bogie converted to an unpowered status, thus leaving a wheel arrangement of A1A-A1A.* **Author's collection**

Below: *The driving controls were significantly changed during the conversion from gas-turbine to electric, as one of the strengths of the conversion was to provide a training model for staff to convert from steam to electric traction; thus the cab is very similar to the original five AC production fleets (AL1-AL5).* **Author's collection**

Above: *Views of E1000 or E2001 actually working trains are very scarce as its operating range was very limited. Most training and testing was carried out between Mauldeth Road and Wilmslow, using empty Mk1 or LMS-designed passenger stock or unfitted freight vehicles. Once the first production AC electric locos started to be delivered and were commissioned, No E2001 was taken out of daily service. No E2001 is seen here at Wilmslow with a training special, alongside a Class AL1 (81) which was in charge of one of many pre-service press and publicity runs to take place in the Manchester area.* **Author's collection**

Above right: *Once sufficient production AC electric locomotives were available the use of No E2001 ceased. It was involved in some aerodynamic tests in the Crewe area and later taken to Scotland for suburban electrification power tests. The locomotive is seen here dumped at Goostrey, shortly prior to being transferred to Rugby for store.* **Author's collection**

Right: *With an old Watford suburban electric unit in the rear, the very decrepit No E2001 is seen dumped outside the Rugby testing station. At one time the locomotive was destined to be involved in further research work involving 25kV overhead power collection, but this work was to be carried out by production classes. No E2001 remained in various sidings in the Rugby area until December 1968 when for the next four years it was stored at Northampton, returning to Rugby in 1972 before being sold for scrap to Cashmore's of Great Bridge.* **Author's collection**

Class 81

Design: AEI/Birmingham RC&W Bo-Bo 25kV/6.25kV overhead AC electric
Number range: E3001-23, E3096/7 (E3301/2), renumbered 81001-22
Introduced: 1959
Withdrawn: 1968-91

Above: *Posed for one of its early official photographs, the pioneer production AL1 class electric No E3001 is shown from its equipment side, identified by the nine air intake grille windows in the side. At this time the locomotive also sported two pantographs, and had the letter code in the first position of the four-character route indicator panel. In keeping with all the original AC locomotives, No E3001 was released to traffic painted in 'electric blue' offset by a white cab roof and window surrounds.* **Author's collection**

When the BTC decided on electrification of the London Midland Region routes from London Euston to Birmingham, Manchester and Liverpool, the order for dual voltage 25kV/6.25kV AC 'production' locomotives was spread over several major builders.

Numerically the first batch, allocated the new AC electric range in the 3000 series, and taking the range from No E3001, was the AL1 fleet, this consisted of 23 passenger or type 'A', and two freight Type 'B' locomotives.

Assembly was carried out by the Birmingham RC&W Co, under contract to AEI. Mechanical design was awarded to BRC&W, who produced a load-bearing structure, formed of girder steel sections, plated in medium-gauge sheet. The exterior body design of all the original AC classes was very much a directive from the BTC design panel, with the individual builders given little personal identity in terms of detail. The body design incorporated a full-width cab at both ends, with electrical equipment housed in interlocked compartments between the cab sections on one side of the structure, a cab-to-cab walkway being provided on the other side.

The entire between-cab or equipment area had a lower than normal height, this was needed to accommodate a roof well for the power collection pantographs, which were electrically arranged to be able to receive power at either 6.25kV or 25kV depending on the area in which the locomotive was used; however, the 6.25kV system was never officially used.

The two body sides of the design were very different; one accommodated four glazed windows (by the cab-cab walkway), while the other incorporated nine ventilation louvre panels.

When built the Type 'A' passenger fleet was numbered in the E3001-23 series, while the Type 'B' freight locomotives were numbered E3301/2, later amended to E3096/7 when it was agreed that all locomotives would form one operational group. Under the 1970s TOPS classification system the fleet became Class 81 and the survivors were renumbered in order 81001-22.

When introduced, in accordance with the BTC Design Committee directive, the livery applied was 'electric blue', off-set with a white cab roof and front window surrounds. After a short period, new demands for track safety necessitated the application of small yellow warning panels, and later full yellow ends were added as standard. Under the 1960s BR traction policy, all-over rail blue with full yellow ends was applied to all class members.

At the time of the design of the 'production' AC fleets vacuum train braking was still the norm, and thus all locos were equipped with a standard vacuum brake system. When the UK railway started the change to two-pipe air braking in the 1960s, the entire fleet was fitted with dual brake equipment, allowing both operation with vacuum and air-fitted stock. At the same time as the air brake equipment was

Above: *A long time prior to the official orders being placed for the original five production classes of AC electric locomotives, the British Transport Commission Design Panel ordered a series of mock-ups to be produced, from which the final exterior and interior designs of the cab would be made. The railway workshops at Doncaster were entrusted with building these highly detailed wooden models. Here we see a full scale front end for the AC design, with a cab end of a Southern Region DC Class HA behind. In terms of the AC locomotive, no provision was made for a four-position route indicator, as for many months during the design period the Southern Region two-digit system was considered. This example sports oval buffers, electric train supply but most surprisingly a steam pipe to the right of the coupling pocket. Red rear tail or marker lights were incorporated.* **Author's collection**

fitted the redundant 6.25kV pantograph was removed with its space taken by the required additional air reservoirs.

At the time of design and introduction the four-character alphanumeric method of train reporting was in use and thus the locomotives incorporated a roller-blind route indicator system on the front end. When originally introduced the blinds had the letter position as the first character; this was later altered to have the letter in the second position with numerals in the first, third and fourth positions. The route indicator boxes were replaced by black screens and white marker 'cut outs' in the mid-1970s following the abolition of train displayed route codes. In later years the redundant indicator boxes were filled in or plated over with two sealed-beam high-intensity marker lights giving frontal indication.

The AL1 fleet in company with the other early modernisation fleets was the mainstay of power for the 1960s LM electrification until

second-generation fleets started to emerge in 1965, being responsible for powering both passenger and freight services. After deployment of Class AL6 and Class 87s, and following the 1970s extension of the LM electrified network to Scotland, the by then Class 81s found work allocated to Shields Electric Depot in Glasgow. The rostering of the fleet, however, still saw members work throughout the AC network. Although a couple of locomotives were withdrawn following accident damage in the 1960s, the majority of fleet members worked for well over 25 years in front line service. Major inroads were made to locomotive numbers commencing in 1988, and the class was eliminated from service by mid-1991.

Thankfully the UK preservation movement did not allow the AL1 fleet to totally disappear. One member, the original No E3003, later TOPS No 81002, has been preserved at Barrow Hill by The AC Locomotive Group.

Above: *After the removal of the redundant second pantograph, and the addition of a small yellow warning end, No E3016 hurries past Tring on 1 May 1966 powering the 14.10 Liverpool Lime Street–Euston express, formed of a mixture of Mk1 and early Mk2 coach designs. This view shows the equipment side of the locomotive and the cast 'Lion holding Wheel' BTC logo in the centre of the bodywork. These aluminium castings are now fetching around £1000 at railway auctions.* **Brian Stephenson**

Below: *From their introduction until withdrawal, Crewe Works was always responsible for the classified attention to the AC locomotive fleets. Regional depot facilities in London, Manchester, Liverpool and later Glasgow dealt with daily attention and service examinations. Showing the revised front end detail, with the former route indicator panel plated over and two sealed beam marker lights inserted, No 81013 is seen in the main erecting shop at BREL Crewe Works on 25 September 1985 receiving a light overhaul. In the background a Class 87 and 86 can be seen.* **Author**

Above: *Following the mid-1970s extension of West Coast electrification from Weaver Junction to Preston, Carlisle and Glasgow, the Class 81 fleet was transferred to Shields Road Depot in Glasgow, from where they were deployed on freight and passenger services. Rostering showed the fleet to be allocated to more freight services than passenger, but this did not stop the fleet from turning up on crack express passenger turns right up to the late 1980s. On 16 July 1986, No 81003 descends Shap Incline at Greenholme powering the 07.40 Glasgow Mossend Yard–Severn Tunnel Junction freight.* **Author**

Below: *With a Class 310 AC EMU on the right about to form a stopping service to Birmingham New Street, Class 81 No 81008 stands at the buffer stops at Euston after arriving with the overnight sleeper service from Glasgow Central on 5 February 1985.* **Author**

Above: *A popular location to find members of the Class 81 fleet in the 1980s was Mossend Yard in Glasgow, close to their Shields Road home depot. Seen from No 1 end, sporting sealed beam marker lights and with a Class 87 in the background, No 81021, the original No E3096 (E3301) type 'B' freight version of the build, was captured on film on 18 June 1983. The locomotive was awaiting a crew change with a southbound engineering train bound for Carlisle.* **Author**

Below: *During the dynamic testing period of the Leyland National bus-bodied Mk1 No DB977091 several high speed runs were undertaken over the West Coast main line. On 30 May 1984, the Leyland test vehicle is the rear coach of this northbound RTC test special passing Milton Keynes powered by Class 81 No 81011 en route from Willesden carriage sidings to Crewe. Other vehicles in the test formation from the front are RDB975136 Lab 12, RDB977089 and RDB975417 Wren.* **Brian Morrison**

Above: *AC electric locomotive maintenance in the London area was performed at a purpose-built facility constructed as part of the 1960s West Coast modernisation. Today, with virtually no electric locomotive operations on the Euston main line, the facility is used for maintenance of local area electric multiple units. In happier days when the depot was a prime source of traction for the Euston routes, No 81007 poses outside the London end of the depot on 7 October 1978.* **Author**

Below: *The pioneer member of the Class AL1 or 81 fleet, No 81001, approaches Wembley Central on 26 June 1973, hauling a five-vehicle Class 3 parcels service bound for Carlisle. At this point the train is traversing the down slow tracks, where the train would probably remain until Rugby, before turning onto the Trent Valley lines via Stafford and Crewe.* **Brian Morrison**

Above: *Much of the early testing and staff training on the production classes of early AC electric locomotives was undertaken in the Manchester area, with most drivers converting from steam to electric traction with a course using No E2001. Very soon after being commissioned, the pioneer member of the production AC fleet, No E3001, passes the huge radio telescope at Jodrell Bank near Goostrey in the Spring of 1960. At this time the change had still to be made to the route display box which shows a letter in the first display position. This locomotive sports standard 'as-built' electric blue livery, offset by a white cab roof and front window surrounds. The buffer beam is finished in red and the underframe in black.* **Author's collection**

Above right: *To provide maintenance facilities for the new London Midland Region main line electric fleet a number of depots were commissioned especially for electric traction. These were principally at Willesden (London), Bletchley (mainly for the EMU fleet, but with loco facilities), Crewe, Longsight (Manchester) and Allerton (Liverpool). Each depot included lines equipped with overhead power supply and deep underside inspection pits. This is a view inside Crewe Electric Depot soon after opening, with three Class AL1s receiving attention, from left to right these are Nos E3001, E3004 and E3002.* **Author's collection**

Right: *Unlike some classes, the AL1s or Class 81s were never the recipients of bright and otherwise interesting colours. All changed from Electric Blue to standard BR corporate rail blue in the 1960s, complete with full yellow warning end, BR double-arrow logo in the middle of the body (these were at first cast and then replaced by white stickers). At the time of renumbering from the 1960s E prefix series to TOPS numbers, the original cast running numbers were replaced with white sticky-backed numerals. Carrying corporate rail blue, No 81012 is seen at Carlisle on 1 April 1989, preparing to depart for Birmingham and Euston with a charter service. The train is formed of preserved Mk1 stock.* **Author**

Class 82

Design: AEI/MV Beyer Peacock Bo-Bo 25kV/6.25kV overhead AC electric
Number range: E3046-55, renumbered 82001-008
Introduced: 1960
Withdrawn: 1969-87

Above: *A rare illustration of the first member of the AL2 fleet, taken at the Gorton factory of Beyer Peacock, and showing the locomotive complete, fully painted and numbered but without the Lion holding Wheel logo on the bodyside. Paperwork shows these were 'delayed in delivery' and caused the first two locomotives to be late in handing over. In common with the first few deliveries of other early AC classes the four-character route indicator displayed letters in the first position for a few months. It is also interesting to see the single arm pantograph raised but with no overhead power lines* in situ. **Author's collection**

Under the original British Transport Commission orders for electric locomotives, a small fleet of 10 Type 'A' (passenger) locomotives was ordered from AEI/Metropolitan-Vickers, this consortium then sub-contracting mechanical design and physical construction to Beyer Peacock of Gorton, Manchester, the builder responsible for the Western Region 'Hymek' Type 3 diesel-hydraulic locomotives.

Under the 1950s BTC electric loco classification system this fleet were allocated the identity AL2 (**AC L**ocomotive Class **2**) and were allocated running numbers in the range E3046 to E3055. Under BR's 1970s TOPS classification the fleet became Class 82, and the survivors numbered 82001-82008.

The first locomotive of the build emerged from Gorton in May 1960, and after a short certification period took up trial running on the Styal line near Manchester, alongside the pioneer electric locomotive No E1000 and 'AL1' No E3001.

The external appearance of the AL2 fleet followed the standard BTC design stipulated for all of the five original orders of classes AL1-AL5, however, on this fleet the construction method was significantly different, using a separate underframe and body assembly. Even in early pre-production planning documentation, it was considered that using this method of construction weight might be something of a problem, and to overcome this alloy and glass fibre was used in the body area.

The between cab equipment bay/walkway layout was similar to

the Class AL1, with the cab layout being to the BTC standard design. All driving controls were provided on the left side of the cab in the direction of travel; brake controls were operated by the driver's left hand, while direction and power operation was operated by the driver's right hand. All instrumentation was on an angled panel, with desk controls either on the display panel or on the desk immediately in front of the driver. A non-driving secondman's seat was provided on the right side of the cab.

Two pantographs were fitted when new, as were vacuum train brakes. In the 1970s, when air-braked rolling stock was being introduced, the fleet was refurbished, incorporating dual brake equipment. The same refurbishment project saw the then redundant second pantograph removed and its space filled by the additional air reservoirs.

In the 'as-built' condition, one side of the AL2 design incorporated six ventilation grilles, while the other had two glazed windows and two ventilation grilles. During refurbishment the grille side was amended to house an additional ventilation panel required for the altered internal equipments.

When originally introduced, the AL2s were allocated to Longsight depot, Manchester, and were used intensely on Manchester-London and Liverpool-London services. In keeping with the BTC directive the fleet displayed standard electric blue livery, offset by white cab roofs and cab window surrounds with a red buffer beam. Over the years small yellow warning ends were applied and then standard corporate rail blue with full yellow warning ends was applied.

The AL2 fleet performed well on the West Coast Main Line and were well liked by staff. However, by 1982-83 the majority of the fleet was deemed as surplus and stored and eventually withdrawn, following the general rationalisation of motive power, reductions in work and the introduction of newer classes.

Slightly better fortunes fell on two examples, Nos 82005 and 82008,

which were retained until 1987 and used on empty stock duties between Wembley carriage sidings and London Euston, being allocated to Willesden depot. This work saw a major change to policy with No 82008 repainted into then standard InterCity/Executive livery.

No 82008 is now preserved by The AC Locomotive Group at Barrow Hill.

Above: *Viewed from the equipment side, the second locomotive of the build No E3047 is seen inside the main erecting shop at Gorton. Using a separate frame and body assembly on this design, weight was always to be a problem and to address this an amount of light weight alloy and fibre glass was used. It is worth noting that although this locomotive was only in its early stages of assembly, the route indicator equipment was already in position.* **Author's collection**

Below: *Awaiting departure from the main 'long' platform at Manchester Piccadilly, the same locomotive as illustrated above, No E3047, makes ready to depart with an inter-regional working to the West Country in the summer of 1961. This train would have given way to diesel haulage at Birmingham New Street.* **Author's collection**

Above: *In the early days of electric running on the West Coast main line, Class AL2 No E3051 approaches the manual level crossing at Marston Green on 8 April 1967 powering the 09.15 London Euston–Liverpool Lime Street via Birmingham service. Note the height of the fully extended pantograph, thus providing suitable clearance for tall road vehicles on crossings.*
Robert Warren

Left: *With a rather 'Heath Robinson' metal plate rivetted over the former route indicator display and two marker lights installed, the 'pioneer' member of the Class 82 fleet, No 82001, awaits departure from Manchester Piccadilly on 10 January 1981 with the 10.45 Manchester–Plymouth service. This locomotive was actually the second of the build, No E3047 as the original first of the fleet No E3046 was withdrawn with accident damage prior to the introduction of TOPS.*
Author

Above: *With its No 1 pantograph end leading, and the route display panel showing an interim black perspex screen with white cut-outs, No 82008 runs into Wembley Yard on 12 May 1980 heading a return empty newspaper train from Manchester. The train was formed of 14 Mk1 BG vans and one passenger vehicle. On the left is a Plasser tamping machine which was working from the Southern Region to Wembley yard. The area in which this illustration was taken is now the European Freight Operations Centre (EFOC).* **Author**

Below: *Until the eventual introduction of push-pull consists and now multiple unit formations, there was always a continued need for locomotives to be available to power empty coaching stock rakes from carriage sidings to the principal London stations. Rather than deploy modern and new resources, some of the 'older' locomotives were retained for these duties in the 1980s. On 13 March 1984, No 82008 is seen 'on the blocks' at Euston with stock for the 07.45 Euston–Glasgow service.* **Author**

Above: *In the 1980s, London Midland diagram staff frequently deployed the 'older' electric classes 81 to 84 onto extra or charter duties, leaving the then core Class 85-87 fleets for the principal rostered services. On 27 March 1982 an additional service from Manchester Piccadilly to London Euston formed entirely of Mk1 stock hurries towards Nuneaton powered by No 82001.* **Author**

Below: *The two Class 82s retained for empty stock workings in the London area after the rest of the fleet was withdrawn, were allocated to Willesden District Electric Depot (DED), where the minimum of maintenance was carried out to keep the pair operational. Painted in Inter-City 'Executive' colours, No 82008 is seen inside Willesden depot along with Class 87 No 87032 and a Class 86. For use on empty stock duties, and long before standard cab-shore radios were mandatory, the two ECS locomotives were fitted with a local radio system, the pick-up of which can be seen fitted on the front end adjacent to the driver's front window, with the wire entering the cab via a hole drilled in the plate over the former route display.* **Author**

Above: *In the days when British Rail offered a Motorail service to transport passengers and their motor cars from London Kensington Olympia to Scotland, Class 82 No 82006 passes Tebay on 12 June 1974 powering service 1S55, formed of seven Mk1s and 11 Motorail flats.* **Brian Morrison**

Below: *For the summer timetable of 1978 a rather unusual 11.03 Tuesdays and Thursdays only service operated from Birmingham New Street to Aberdeen. The train formed of Mk1 stock was powered by an AC electric as far as Mossend, from where a Class 47 took over for the remainder of the journey. With No 82005 at the helm, the service approaches Carlisle on 3 August 1978.* **Brian Morrison**

Above: *For a period in the mid-1970s when the British Railways Board decreed that the use of four-position route indicators on trains was to end, most depots set the indicators to display four '0's until the blinds and glass could be removed and replaced by sealed-beam marker lights. On 3 March 1979, No 82006 passes West London Junction, adjacent to Willesden District Electric Depot and Willesden Junction station, powering a charter special from Manchester to Euston.* **Author**

Below: *The UK automotive industry used to use the rail industry to transport a considerable number of finished motor cars in the 1960s-80s period, with regular timetabled services from the principal manufacturing sites. On 6 March 1978, No 82002 approaches Norton Bridge near Crewe with a train of new Ford products from the Halewood assembly plant in Liverpool bound for London.* **N. Johnston**

Above: *Still devoid of its 'Lion holding Wheel' cast bodyside logo, No E3046 is shown at the head of an unfitted freight train in the Wilmslow area. The text on the rear of this illustration indicates this was the first powered move of this locomotive after delivery the short distance from Beyer Peacock; it is also noted that after the active tests the locomotive returned to the builders for 'completion'. The livery is standard BTC electric blue with white cab roof and window surrounds plus a red buffer beam.* **Author's collection**

Below: *Now owned by The AC Locomotive Group, No 82008 has been saved for further generations of enthusiasts to understand the development of AC main-line traction in the UK. In virtually ex-works BR rail blue livery, No 82008 shares depot space with a Class 90 and 92 at Crewe International Depot on 18 October 1994.* **Author**

Class 83

Design: English Electric Bo-Bo 25kV/6.25kV overhead AC electric
Number range: E3024-35, 3098-9 (E3303/4), renumbered 83001-015
Introduced: 1960
Withdrawn: 1975-89

Above: *A front three-quarter view of the third locomotive of the build, No E3026. This view is from the main equipment side housing four large ventilation grilles to provide a cooling air supply for electrical equipment. This locomotive sports the standard number, letter, number, number route display. In common with the other first-generation classes, both pantographs were able to operate at either 6.25kV AC or 25kV AC. On-board detection equipment automatically changed-over the transforming equipment.* **Author's collection**

The BTC Class AL3 order was for 15 locomotives. This was originally a split order, covering 12 Type 'A' (passenger) and three Type 'B' (freight) locomotives, but during the course of assembly this was amended to 13 Type 'A' and two Type 'B'.

The contract for this batch was awarded to English Electric, who sub-contracted design and assembly to Vulcan Foundry at Newton-le-Willows.

The main structural assembly was formed of a load-bearing unit, assembled out of 'Corten' steel - the main underframe was an integral load-bearing unit. The body structure was formed of a frame onto which medium gauge steel plate was fitted, the equipment bay roof was formed out of fibre glass to keep weight to a minimum, while the cab roofs were finished in steel.

The internal layout followed the standard BTC directive for AC traction, with a walkway on one side, and interlocked electrical compartments or bays on the other.

An obvious problem of requiring a cab-cab full-length internal walkway on a locomotive fitted with a pantograph was restricted roof height. On this build this was partially overcome by incorporating a recessed walkway floor.

Bodyside ventilation was provided in the equipment bays by four grille panels, while the walkway had three glazed windows; following refurbishment and the fitting of revised electrical equipment, extra internal ventilation was needed and the middle window on the walkway side was adapted to provide an additional grille.

The Vulcan Foundry workshop commenced assembly of the first Type 'A' locomotives in November 1959, with No E3024 handed over

to the BTC in July 1960; the final Type 'A', No E3035, was released to traffic just one year later. The Type 'B' locomotives were built in 1961, taking much longer to assemble. To differentiate between passenger and freight locomotives, the first two Type 'Bs' were initially numbered in the E33xx series as E3303 and E3304.

In 1960 the main voice behind AC electric traction at the time in the UK, English Electric entered discussion with and sought permission from the British Transport Commission to build the final locomotive of the order with advanced power and control equipment. With the BTC by then keen on developing electric traction and interested in exploring new and novel traction principles, this permission was granted. This then led to a major engineering development stage with the installation of a silicon rectifier, together with rheostatic brake equipment in place of the standard equipment.

Under the original order contract, the final locomotive was to have been a Type 'B' freight machine, but as test equipment was installed, in the process of developing the next generation of AC power, the BTC agreed to make this an additional passenger or Type 'A' locomotive, allocated the number E3100. To provide ventilation for the new equipment, this locomotive had a number of minor alterations to its bodyside grilles.

In keeping with all the early first generation AC classes, the AL3s were fitted with two pantographs; however, at the same time as the installation of dual brake equipment, one pantograph was removed, its space filled with extra air reservoirs.

Standard BTC electric blue, complete with white window surrounds and cab roof was applied to all locomotives when built. By the late 1960s this had given way to standard corporate rail blue

Right: *A view taken inside the Vulcan Foundry workshops at Newton-le-Willows, the birthplace of so many UK and indeed overseas locomotives, we see the bodyshell of the first of the AL3 fleet taking shape. This view is from the walkway (window) side and clearly shows the frame construction prior to cladding with medium-gauge steel plate.* **Author's collection**

with full yellow warning ends. Under the 1970s TOPS classification system the AL3s became Class 83, and were renumbered in the range 83001 - 83015.

When first introduced, in keeping with most English Electric products, the fleet gave excellent service, with very few on-line failures. However, by the late 1960s the fleet was causing a number of problems, mainly involving the power equipment. The problems became so severe that by 1970 the BRB authorised the entire fleet to be stored, with many people in the industry considering that the fleet would be withdrawn. However, authorisation for electrification of the WCML north from Weaver Junction to Glasgow reversed the position, as a great need was foreseen for extra AC locomotives.

New locomotives (Class 87s) were in the course of production, but extra power would be needed, thus, the Class 83s were refurbished.

By 1982, when new traction had settled in and service rationalisation had taken place, the fleet was again condemned, this time officially being shown as 'surplus to requirements'. At first the fleet was stored but with no further use on the horizon, all were withdrawn.

Two examples, Nos 83003 and 83012, were, however, retained for empty stock operations between Wembley and London Euston, operating until 1988 and being withdrawn in 1989.

No 83012 is now preserved by The AC Locomotive Group and is presently at Barrow Hill, painted in 1960s electric blue.

Right: *The final built Class AL3, No E3100, which was fitted with advanced power and control equipment using silicon rectifiers and incorporated regenerative braking, was used by English Electric as a structural test bed prior to fitting out. After the shell was completed at Vulcan Foundry, it was taken to the English Electric Structural Testing Station at Whetstone, Leicestershire between June 1960 and February 1961 where the integrity of the body was evaluated using a compression rig. The shell is shown wired up for testing, note all the data recording points on the cab side and walkway bodyside just behind the cab door area.* **Author's collection**

Above: *When complete and handed over to the BTC, No E3100 was the subject of extensive static and dynamic testing on the West Coast route, especially in terms of its regenerative brake equipment. Traversing the four track section of the Euston–Crewe route near Stafford, No E3100 leads a joint BTC/English Electric test train formed of recording vehicles and three further Class AL3s, added to the formation as weight and power 'pull' from the overhead power line.*
Author's collection

Left: *With a mixed collection of LMS and BR origin stock behind, No E3024 awaits departure from Manchester Piccadilly station soon after introduction with a service bound for Birmingham. At this time no yellow warning panel had been added to the original 'electric blue' livery.*
Author's collection

Above: *Built as No E3030 in October 1960, this locomotive was renumbered 83007 in December 1972 under the computer-based TOPS reporting system. On 11 June 1974 it is seen passing near Oxenholme, powering a southbound parcels train including at least one Travelling Post Office (TPO) vehicle coupled directly behind the locomotive. No 83007 was finally withdrawn in August 1983 and broken up by Vic Berry, Leicester, a year later.* **Brian Morrison**

Below: *Viewed passing over the Euston Suburban DC electrified lines between Willesden and Wembley, Class 83 No 83010 heads north towards Wembley powering a Freightliner service from Willesden Freightliner Terminal on 13 September 1979.* **Les Bertram**

Above: *Photographed in the corporate BR rail blue era following refurbishment, No 83006 hurries past Nuneaton on 27 March 1982 leading the 07.30 Manchester Piccadilly–London Euston relief service. Just to the right of the Class 83 the front of a 'Peak' running around a Nottingham–Wembley charter can be seen. No 83006 sports the post route-indicator black screen with white cut-outs for frontal illumination.* **Author**

Below: *While the author was performing secondman's duties on 'Crompton' No 33009 on 8 March 1979, his duty took him and his driver to Mitre Bridge Junction, to relieve Class 83 No 83010 on a military charter from Appleby to Aldershot. Mitre Bridge Junction was then the extremity of the 25kV electrified network with just sufficient room to detach and run forward through the crossover and return to Willesden DED. This view of No 83010 shows the revised walkway side body structure following refurbishment with a grille in the former centre window position.* **Author**

Above: *Front end comparison between Class 83 No 83008 on the left and BR-built Class 85 No 85036 on the right. Although looking very similar a number of angular and detail differences can be seen, as well as the paint application style which also changes the overall appearance of the locomotive. This view was taken at Willesden Yard on 12 May 1980.* **Author**

Below: *Viewed from the window side, No 83015 departs from Carlisle on 26 January 1980, having taken over from diesel traction while powering the 09.40 (SO) Leicester–Glasgow Central service, which had travelled north on that day via the Settle & Carlisle route.* **Brian Morrison**

Above: *Introduced in July 1961, No 83012 emerges from Primrose Hill Tunnel on 6 June 1973 hauling a Euston-bound express. The aluminium BR arrow logo is still displayed in raised fashion on the bodysides but the TOPS five digit number has been applied in white transfer to replace the original cast numbers.* **Brian Morrison**

Below: *The pioneer member of the Class 83 fleet, No 83001, travels south past the site of the old Bushey water troughs on 29 April 1978, hauling a Freightliner service bound for Willesden.* **Brian Morrison**

Above & Below: *A pair of very interesting comparison illustrations. The view above of No E3028 shows the locomotive posed outside the test house at Vulcan Foundry, Newton-le-Willows painted in BTC electric blue with white cab roof and window frames. It shows the three window or walkway side of the locomotive, with the 'Lion holding Wheel' central on the bodyside. The illustration below shows preserved No E3035 (83012) restored to 'original' condition by The AC Locomotive Group at Barrow Hill, the locomotive is seen here on display at Old Oak Common open day and shows the equipment or grille side of the bodywork. The only real difference between the two is that the preserved locomotive shows dual brake equipment and only one roof-mounted pantograph.* **Author's collection/Author**

Class 84

Design: North British Locomotive/GEC Bo-Bo 25kV/6.25kV overhead AC electric
Number range: E3036-45, renumbered to 84001-010
Introduced: 1960
Withdrawn: 1977-80

Above: *With its alpha route code in the first position, AL4 No E3036 is seen on the Styal line soon after delivery from Glasgow. The slightly recessed route indicator box, together with oval buffers gave this small fleet immediate recognition when seen from the lineside. Also in keeping with NBL tradition, cast diamond-shaped makers plates were fitted below the driver's side running number. This view shows the walkway side of the locomotive with four grilles and two fixed glazed windows. The livery is standard BTC electric blue with white cab roof and window surrounds.* **Author's collection**

The 10 locomotives ordered by the BTC as the AL4 fleet were all of Type 'A' (passenger) and constructed by the North British Locomotive Co of Glasgow, under contract to GEC who were awarded the main build project.

NBL decided to use an integral structure with all steel members, unlike other builders who used fibre glass for some body parts to reduce weight.

Construction of the locomotives started in mid-1959, with the first, No E3036, handed over to the BTC in March 1960. The style of the build and livery followed the BTC main directive, but incorporated a slightly recessed route indicator panel, giving an immediate method of recognition of the NBL batch. Also, oval buffers were fitted rather than the conventional round type.

The between-cab layout followed the standard style, with equipment bays on one side and a cab-cab walkway on the other. The walkway side had four aluminium frame drop-light windows, the only openable equipment room windows fitted to the AC classes. On the equipment side, four grille panels and two fixed glazed windows were fitted.

The number range allocated to the fleet was E3036-45; under TOPS the fleet became Class 84 and was renumbered 84001-010.

Upon introduction the fleet was allocated to Manchester Longsight,

but sadly, problems were soon encountered with both rough riding and failures of the power equipment. In April 1963 the entire fleet was temporarily taken out of service and sent to GEC Dukinfield where remedial work was carried out. Regrettably, even when the class returned to service after this work, electrical problems were still encountered, eventually leading to nine members of the fleet being stored at Bury Depot in 1967; the other locomotive, No E3043 was sent to the Rugby test station for trials.

At the time it seemed that the AL4 fleet was doomed to be some of the shortest lived main-line locos. However, after authorisation for the extension of the WCML electrification to Scotland there was a pressing need for additional electric locomotives, and this was fulfilled by refurbishing the Class 84 fleet at BREL Doncaster, which was completed in 1972. As part of the refurbishment, dual brake equipment was fitted and the second pantograph removed.

After refurbishment, many of the previous problems were overcome, but others were soon identified, mainly involving the traction motor drives. Expenditure on the fleet was largely curtailed by the mid-1970s, as the BRB could not authorise any further investment in such a small fleet. By 1977 the first withdrawals were made, with the entire class withdrawn by 1980.

The AC Electrics

Two members of the class were saved from immediate scrap. No E3044 (84009) was rebuilt as a mobile load bank and operated by the Mechanical & Electrical Engineer's department in Derby, it was renumbered as ADB968021 and used for testing of new and upgraded overhead line equipment. The mobile load bank was withdrawn from use in the autumn of 1992 and broken up.

No E3036 (84001) has a slightly happier after-use life, for it was saved by the National Railway Museum, York and placed on display in the Great Hall. After a few years it was loaned to The AC Locomotive Group at Barrow Hill, where it remains at the time of writing.

Above & Below: *According to the traffic notice of the period, the route display T--4 was used on many early trial runs with the AL4 locomotives; it is assumed to mean 'Test AL4'. In the above view locomotive No E3037 passes the radio telescope at Jodrell Bank near Goostrey powering a very mixed rake of LMS-designed stock. In the view below, No E3036 is seen on the Styal line heading an unfitted freight. The original test runs for all of the first generation classes involved driver training operating the various classes at the head of vacuum brake fitted passenger stock and loose coupled freight vehicles.* Both: **Author's collection**

Left: With 'T2' as its train reporting number, No E3036 in 'as delivered' condition is seen at Wilmslow on 21 July 1960 while taking part in a driver training run formed of unfitted freight stock. **Alan H. Bryant**

Below left: Although the London Midland Region AC electric fleet was allocated on paper to Willesden, Longsight, Allerton, Crewe Electric and Glasgow Shields, other maintenance facilities also took part in overhaul and servicing. Crewe Diesel Depot housed a wheel lathe, and frequently AC class members would be hauled there from the electric depots for tyre attention. On 23 July 1975, No 84007 is seen inside Crewe Diesel Depot in the company of a Class 50 and a Class 24 awaiting its turn on the wheel re-profile lathe. **Author**

Below: Formed of a complete rake of blue and grey BR InterCity Mk2 stock, the pioneer member of the class No 84001, which is now part of the National Collection but outbased at Barrow Hill and looked after by AC Locomotive Group, heads down the West Coast Main Line near Carpenders Park on 29 April 1978 powering a joint DEG/DAA 'North West Rambler' charter. **Brian Morrison**

Above: *The final member of the build, No 84010 is seen passing Rowell, Cumbria, powering a southbound automotive train formed of the then BR standard 'Cartic-4' wagons on 19 September 1978. By this time the four '0' display on the route indicator had become the norm.* **Dave Canning**

Below: *Following conversion into a Mobile Load Bank at the Engineering Development Unit (EDU) Derby, Class 84 No 84009 was renumbered into the departmental series as ADB968021. The modification work to create a load bank was a major undertaking with a large bank of electrical resistances installed at one end, requiring some structural alterations to provide adequate ventilation on both body side and roof. During its period of line testing on the then newly-electrified East Coast Main Line, No ADB968021 is seen at York on 27 July 1990. Note the small headlight on the front end and the application of RTC red and blue livery.* **Author**

Class 85

Design: BR Workshops/AEI Bo-Bo 25kV/6.25kV overhead AC electric
Number range: E3056-95, renumbered 85001-040, 85101-114
Introduced: 1961
Withdrawn: 1983-92

Above: *The BR Workshops-built Class AL5s were always identifiable from the other pioneering electric classes by the near-solid block of ventilation grilles along the equipment side. Here No E3070 is seen at Stafford powering a three-vehicle overhead line inspection train in 1962. With a fleet of 40 locomotives, the AL5s became the standard first-generation AC electric until the 100-strong Class AL6 or Class 86 fleet emerged in the mid-1960s. In common with all of the original orders, electric blue with white cab roof and window surrounds was applied when built.* **Author's collection**

The order for the largest number of locomotives from one builder made under the original LM electrification plan was a batch of 40 AL5 locomotives. This was placed with the then BR Workshops Division, which allocated assembly work to Doncaster. Power, control and other technical equipment was supplied by GEC/AEI.

When introduced the AL5s were allocated the number range E3056-95; under the TOPS classification scheme, this was amended to Class 85 with the number range 85001-040.

Structural design of this fleet followed more traditional methods; the base underframe was formed from seven box sections, on to which the cab sections and lower body portion was assembled, thus forming a trough-shaped fabrication. A lightweight top body section was then fitted on to the trough to form the body shell.

One feature of this batch, and very important for maintenance, was that the complete upper body section between the cabs was removable; this was especially useful for major equipment replacement of components such as the transformer.

The internal between-cab style followed the AL1-AL4 design with equipment to one side and a walkway on the other. The equipment bodyside housed 10 ventilation louvres, while the walkway side has four glazed windows.

When introduced the then standard two roof-mounted pantographs were installed, but in later years, after dual voltage equipment was removed and air brake equipment was fitted, the second pantograph was removed.

The Doncaster 'Plant' works commenced production of the AL5s in February 1960, completing the first locomotive the following October, when No E3056 was exhibited at the Electrification Conference Exhibition at Battersea, London.

After a few early teething problems the AL5s (Class 85s) settled down to give excellent all-round service, spending much of their operational period allocated to the purpose-built Crewe Electric Depot.

Standard BTC electric blue was applied when built, but this gave way to corporate BR rail blue in the mid-1960s, complete with full yellow warning ends. By the time this build emerged, the standard configuration of route indicator digit positions had been established, so from new these had number, letter, number, number positions.

The Class 85s operated for many years as the backbone of WCML electrified services, operating alongside the AL6 (Class 86s) working a full range of services ranging from express passenger to light pick-up freight. The class remained in front line service until mid-1991, although inroads were made into the fleet from 1989.

A slight twist in the class history came in 1989, when 14 examples were modified by Crewe Electric depot for freight-only operation. Their maximum speed was reduced to 80mph, train heat equipment was removed and a reduced maintenance schedule introduced due to the lower mileages operated. These locomotives were reclassified as Class 85/1 and numbered in the series 85101-114.

Towards the later years of the locomotives' general operation, they

Above: *Under the London Midland Region's 1960s modernisation plan, a District Electric Depot (DED) to serve Merseyside was built at Allerton. This was a multi-purpose structure and also maintained the local area's diesel locomotive and multiple-unit fleets. Two tracks inside the state-of-the-art building were dedicated to electric locomotive attention, being equipped with underside inspection pits but not, however, fitted with overhead power lines. AL5 No E3063 with three other first generation electrics and a DMU are seen inside the shed in June 1962.* **Author's collection**

all became more extensively used on freight duties, mainly over the northern section of the WCML especially between Mossend and Crewe, while a small number was dedicated to empty passenger stock operations in the London and Manchester areas.

No major structural changes befell this fleet, except the replacement of the original four-character route indicator boxes with sealed beam marker lights from the early 1980s.

One locomotive of this fleet remains; No 85006 (85101) was saved from scrap and is now owned by The AC Locomotive Group and is preserved at Barrow Hill Museum.

Below: *To split up the 25kV AC overhead network into manageable power sections, a number of 'no power' neutral sections were built into the network. When approaching one of these neutral sections, the train's driver would 'run off' power to avoid drawing an arc when leaving the powered cable. Class AL5 No E3065 is seen approaching a neutral section on the four-track section of the West Coast Main Line near Tamworth in autumn 1964, where BICC had installed a modified glass fibre/ceramic bead section in the catenary.* **Author's collection**

Above: *After refurbishment, fitting of dual brake equipment and marker lights in place of the headcode box and repainting in corporate BR rail blue, No 85012 passes Blackrigg, north of Carlisle on 8 June 1979 powering a Glasgow–Carlisle empty van service, formed of a variety of BR, LMS and even Southern design stock.* **Author**

Below: *With the photographer eagerly waiting the passing of the northbound passenger train, Class 85 No 85018 hurries down Shap incline at Greenholme on a snowy 9 February 1983, while heading a Mossend to Bescot air brake freight service.* **Author**

Above: *The early AC electric locomotives were often called 'roarers' by enthusiasts after the roaring sound emitted when taking power. Roaring well, No 85010 passes Greenholme on 4 June 1979 leading a heavy rake of 'Cartic' wagons loaded with new Ford cars bound for Scotland. This slightly elevated view clearly shows the additional roof mounted air tanks added when dual brake equipment was fitted.* **Author**

Right: *In the 1970s and 1980s double heading with AC classes was never common, mainly due to their superior hauling power when compared with diesel classes. However, on 7 August 1980, No 82004, rostered to power a Blackpool—Crewe local service forward from Preston, was in trouble, and was assisted forward from Warrington by Class 85 No 85026. The train is seen at Crewe where the '85' was removed and returned to Warrington and the '82' taken to Crewe depot for repair.* **Author**

Above: *After the introduction of the Railfreight ABS (Air Braked Service) network, the Class 85 fleet was frequently used on these trains. Here a northbound ABS from Willesden to Carlisle hurries past Hest Bank on 8 February 1983 led by No 85033, with its 'walkway' side nearest the camera. The train is an interesting collection of international bogie tanks at the front with an amazing collection of four-wheel box vans towards the centre; these were rebuilt from vacuum stock in the late 1970s.* **Author**

Below: *With a short Euston to Crewe parcels service, No 85006 makes a brief stop at Rugby on 2 March 1984 to off-load just a handful of items. The sealed-beam marker lights can be seen to good advantage; it is surprising that when these locomotives were built no form of frontal illumination was provided.* **Author**

Above: *By the 1990s the Class 85 fleet saw little passenger work, with numerous Class 86s, 87s and 90s available to operators. On 30 March 1990, No 85030 was rostered for a front line duty, when it powered the 14.20 Friday only relief service from Crewe to Edinburgh, seen passing Holme in Cumbria.* **Author**

Below: *With the modification of 14 Class 85s for freight use, almost at the same time as UK freight traffic was in terminal decline, the full deployment of this class was never seen. On 19 November 1990, No 85103 traverses the northbound slow line at Carpenders Park leading just two side opening cargo wagons as the afternoon Willesden Brent Yard to Crewe Basford Hall ABS service.* **Author**

Above: *Powering a Mossend to Warrington Air Braked Service (ABS), No 85016 nears Gretna, the border between Scotland and England, on 5 June 1979. This lengthy train is formed of eight limestone hoppers, six chemical tanks from the ICI fleet and seven covered open wagons carrying military cargo.* **Author**

Left: *With an obvious broken bulb in the left side marker light, No 85022 makes ready to depart from Manchester Piccadilly on 3 October 1981 with the 18.12 service to Euston. Coupled directly behind the locomotive is a buffet car, which was out of use and being transferred from Manchester Longsight to Willesden.* **Author**

The AC Electrics

Above: *Modified Class 85/1 No 85108 approaches Stafford on 24 October 1989 leading a Carlisle–Willesden empty van and TPO service, after working north overnight as the London—Carlisle Travelling Post Office service.* **Author**

Below: *At first sight this looks like a very uneconomic train, formed of just empty flats; however, it was a stock transfer move of repaired Freightliner flats from Crewe to Willesden Freightliner terminal. The transfer trip is seen passing Carpenders Park on the 'up' slow line on 19 November 1990 powered by Class 85/1 No 85102.* **Author**

Above: *With the beautiful Cumbrian mountains as a backdrop covered in freshly fallen snow, Class 85 No 85038 passes Grayrigg on 9 February 1983 leading the 08.23 Glasgow/09.06 Edinburgh to Nottingham service.* **Author**

Left: *Waiting between duties at Crewe on the night of 3 October 1981, No 85012 is seen from its equipment side No 2 end. Although the livery was 'modernised' with stick-on TOPS running numbers in the 1970s, the cast BR double-arrow logo remained.* **Author**

Below: *End of the road! Crewe Electric Depot became the final dumping ground for the majority of withdrawn AL1 to AL5 locomotives, prior to disposal to private scrap dealers or being broken up by BR. The vast majority of AC electrics were broken up by MC Metal Processors, Glasgow.* **Author**

Above: *Thankfully one member of the Class 85 fleet, No 85101 (85006), the original E3061, has been saved for preservation and is in the hands of the AC Locomotive Group, based at Barrow Hill. The locomotive is seen in 'as withdrawn' condition at Exeter Riverside on 30 April 1994 during an open weekend in company with 'Dutch' Class 31 No 31105.* **Author**

Below: *Carrying 1970s corporate BR rail blue livery, complete with full yellow warning end and window surrounds with sealed beam marker lights, No 85003 awaits the right away from the station staff and the green flag from the guard to re-start the 13.26 Manchester Piccadilly to Birmingham New Street service from Stafford on 23 March 1988. The train is formed of a mix of Mk1 and Mk2 stock painted in then standard blue and grey livery.* **Author**

Class 86

Design: BR Workshops/English Electric Bo-Bo 25kV overhead AC electric
Number range: E3101-3200, renumbered to 86001-902 (in batches)
Introduced: 1965
Withdrawn: from 1986

Above: *Painted in early BR blue with a full yellow warning end, but still retaining the 'Lion holding Wheel' cast logo on the mid-body side, No E3178 stands at Liverpool Lime Street at the head of the Liverpool Pullman stock. The Class 3 route indicator is slightly inappropriate for this train. This view shows the 'as built' condition with original un-cluttered front end, original bogies and route indicator display.* **Author**

The AL6 or Class 86 fleet was the single largest order ever placed for electric locos in the UK, consisting of 100 locomotives, which represented the BRB's second generation of main line electric traction.

The order was placed in 1963 with English Electric/AEI to supply internal equipment, while mechanical construction was divided between English Electric's subsidiary Vulcan Foundry in Newton-le-Willows and the BR workshops at Doncaster. The building split emerged due to the tight timescale in which the BTC required the fleet in traffic.

The basic design was developed from the first generation AL1-AL5 types, but much of the internal equipment was revised; this was done to introduce the latest in terms of technology as well as to improve the layout. External body alterations saw revision of the cab end design to incorporate a flat lower panel, and raked-back front screens. The equipment side of the design incorporated nine grille panels, while the walkway side had four air grilles and two glazed windows. By the time the AL6s were ordered the 6.25kV system was being abolished and thus the AL6 fleet was for 25kV operation only and fitted with just one pantograph.

A complete change from first-generation designs came in traction equipment, which consisted of axle-hung rather than frame-mounted traction motors. At the design stage it was considered these would give an improved ride over the frame-mounted type, but in practice this was far from the case. Class 86 traction motor and bogie problems eventually led to serious bogie frame fractures and conributed to track damage. To overcome this problem newly designed 'Flexicoil' suspension bogies were fitted on an experimental basis from the early 1970s, and progressively to the entire fleet, as were low track-force wheel sets.

In the period of advanced planning for the next generation of electric locomotives in the early 1970s, three Class 86s were rebuilt as Class 87 test-beds, fitted with projected Class 87 bogies, which incorporated fully spring-borne traction motors, revised traction equipment was also fitted.

When originally introduced, the AL6 design was painted in electric blue, which on the first few examples released to traffic did not have a yellow warning panel. Over the years full yellow ends were applied and the blue amended to the corporate BR scheme.

After introduction of the various new business sectors under BR in the 1980s, InterCity colours in various schemes appeared, with the

Right: *A handful of early releases from EE Vulcan Foundry in Newton-le-Willows emerged painted in all-over electric blue (a slightly different version that that applied to the pioneering classes of AL1-AL5), offset by a white cab roof and window surrounds. Sporting a cross-arm pantograph, No E3157 is seen between Stafford and Crewe in December 1966 with a three coach power collection test train.* **Author's collection**

standard 'swallow' scheme applied from 1988. A unique repaint to No 86401 took place in 1988, when Network SouthEast colours were applied; over the years the fleet has worn a vast number of different colour schemes, as illustrated on the following pages.

As the sectorisation of BR spread in the late-1980s/early-1990s, leading up to privatisation, further livery variations emerged, including Railfreight triple grey and Rail express systems red to name but two.

From their original deployment, the area of operation of this fleet changed considerably over the years. When first introduced the entire fleet of 100 operated on the West Coast Main Line, allocated to Willesden DED. Their operating range first increased in the mid-1970s following electrification north of Weaver Junction to Glasgow. By the mid-1980s after East Anglia electrification was complete, Class 86s were deployed on Liverpool Street-Norwich duties at first allocated to Ilford and later Norwich Crown Point. The '86' fleet gave sterling service on this route, not being displaced until 2005 by Class 90s.

With the privatisation of the railway in the mid-1990s, the Class 86 fleet was split between the passenger and freight operators, with the locos passing to leasing companies. Virgin Trains became the operator of a sizeable fleet for West Coast and CrossCountry services, with Anglia Railways (later 'one Railway') retaining the Norwich route fleet.

On the freight side, locomotives became operated by EWS and Freightliner. With all the changes to the network, each of the new operators wanted to make their 'mark' and a number of new liveries emerged.

After the various fleet modification programmes were carried out, five sub-classes exist within the Class 86 fleet: 86/1 — Class 87 test-bed locomotives, 86/2 — general passenger fleet fitted with Flexicoil suspension and GEC 282BZ traction motors, 86/4 — locomotives

operated by EWS for Royal Mail or charter traffic and fitted with Flexicoil suspension and GEC 282AZ traction motors, 86/5 — a one-off sub-class operated by Freightliner, fitted with revised gearing (this was the second use of the 86/5 grouping; it was originally used in the 1980s for freight-dedicated locomotives), and 86/6 — locomotives used by Freightliner with their electric train supply equipment isolated.

In common with all main line classes, headlights were fitted from the mid 1990s, while redundant four-character route indicator boxes were plated over and removed, being replaced by sealed beam marker lights and later high-power headlights.

When built, no form of multiple control was installed. During the mid-1980s Time Division Multiplex (TDM) jumpers of the RCH style were fitted to most examples, as were standard multiple control jumpers to the Class 86/4 and 86/6 fleet which by mid-1992 started to be removed as the TDM system became more satisfactory and standard.

Following resurrection of the railway naming policy in the 1970s the majority of the Class were named, mainly using cast standard style plates.

The end of mainstream passenger work for the class came with the introduction of new Virgin Trains traction for West Coast and CrossCountry operations. With a full Voyager and Pendolino service operating, the only passenger route to retain Class 86 operation was on the Anglia main line between Liverpool Street and Norwich. The freight sector kept the class going for a little longer, but by the early 2000s EWS had withdrawn all their class members, with Freightliner retaining a handful for intermodal train operations.

Sadly by 2006 a considerable number of class members have been broken up for scrap while others remain stored. A small number have been preserved.

Right: *This view of the main erecting shop at Vulcan Foundry shows six class members under construction in late 1966. It clearly shows how the top section of the bodywork was a separate unit and provided uninterrupted access to the main equipment bays. At the far end of the shop on the right is an upperbody assembly being fitted out, while a near-complete locomotive is seen in the centre of the shop. This locomotive carries the identity No 16 on its left buffer; as this has a yellow end, it must presumably be production No 16 of the second batch built at Vulcan (E3141-E3160) which became No E3156.* **Author's collection**

Above: *Taken during the route indicator transition period, when four '0's were displayed, un-named Class 86/2 No 86261 starts the climb of Shap incline at Greenholme with the 07.45 Euston–Glasgow service on 6 June 1979, soon after loco-hauled Mk3 stock was introduced on the route. At this time a number of electric locomotives of various classes sported a slight space in their number between the class and actual running identity.* **Author**

Below: *Taken at the same location as the upper illustration on this page but of a southbound train, recently named Class 86/2 No 86241* Glenfiddich *heads south over Shap incline on 4 June 1979 powering a vacuum-fitted freight bound for Warrington. This locomotive was already modified with sealed beam marker lights and sports a cross-arm pantograph. Note where the original BR double-arrow logo has been painted over to apply the name.* **Author**

Above: *To provide driver-train communication as well as a method of control for Driving Van Trailers (DVTs), Class 86/2s were progressively fitted with RCH jumper cables in the 1980. After transfer to Ilford for Liverpool Street–Norwich use, No 86260* Driver Wallace Oakes GC *passes through Stratford Station in East London on 14 April 1989 leading the 12.30 Liverpool Street to Norwich. This illustration was taken in the days before fixed formations and DBSOs were introduced.* **Author**

Below: *Although originally built without any facility for multiple operation, following the extension of the West Coast electrification to Glasgow in the mid-1970s and the deployment of class members on heavy freight services, multiple control equipment was installed on many locomotives. Class 86/4 No 86434* University of London *fitted with both RCH and multiple control jumpers works in multiple with Class 87 No 87032* Kenilworth *on 2 March 1989 powering a northbound Freightliner service past South Kenton.* **Author**

Above: *Painted in InterCity 'Swallow' livery with RCH jumpers and standard headlight, No 86216 passes Plumpton near Carlisle with the 09.24 Edinburgh to Birmingham service on 17 September 1992.* **Author**

Left: *The three members of Class 86/1 modified to test Class 87 equipment were the first AC electrics to carry quartz headlights, shown on No 86103 at Carlisle on 18 July 1986 leading the 15.45 Euston—Glasgow. The locomotive is painted in 'Executive' livery.* **Author**

Below: *Following privatisation and the use of the majority of the '86' fleet by Virgin Trains, their red and grey livery was applied to most examples. No 86231* Starlight Express *departs from Edinburgh with a CrossCountry service to Plymouth on 14 November 1999.* **Author**

Above: *Following the formation of Rail express systems in October 1991, the red corporate livery with blue and grey flecks was applied to their traction. Here Class 86/4 No 86430* Saint Edmund *is seen in use on the Anglia main line at Ipswich on 31 January 1997.* **Author**

Right: *Painted in Rail express systems red but without the decals, No 86241* Glenfiddich *is seen on Shap incline on 16 September 1992 forming a southbound Royal Mail service bound for Warrington.* **Author**

Below: *After privatisation of the UK rail network from the mid-1990s came many new liveries. One was Freightliner, who branded their triple-grey Class 86s with the company logo, shown here on Class 86/6 No 86623 which also sports oval buffers and shows 'patches' where multiple jumpers have been removed.* **Author**

Left: *In the late 1960s and early 1970s BR Research in their quest for additional information on aerodynamics on train designs produced a fibreglass 'cone' which was attached to Class 86 No E3173, which was already the pioneer of 'Flexicoil' bogie technology. It operated a number of test runs over the LM main line at speeds up to 125mph, and from this research the body style for the APT and HST was developed. No E3173 is seen near Tring on 25 October 1970.* **Colin Gifford**

Right: *Showing the original 'as built' electric blue without a yellow warning panel, as applied to a small number of 1965 and early 1966 deliveries from Vulcan Foundry. No E3161 was the first of the Vulcan batch, and is seen in the works yard awaiting delivery.* **Author's collection**

Right: *Originally all major attention to AC electric locomotives was carried out at Crewe Works, however changing maintenance practices saw this work shared with other facilities from the early 1990s, including Stratford, Doncaster and Glasgow. On 2 May 1995, No 86250* The Glasgow Herald *is seen inside the stripping shop at RML Doncaster being prepared for a general overhaul.* **Author**

Left: *The Class 86 driving cab layout was very well designed. The previous experience of the five earlier designs was incorporated, together with major input from the drivers' trade union ASLEF and drivers themselves. In the usual style, brake controls were operated by the left hand, and power controller and master switch by the right hand. Here traction inspector John Thompson takes the controls of No 86204 while powering an Edinburgh—Reading train on 6 June 1996.* **Author**

Right: *As Virgin Trains' contribution to the 150th anniversary celebrations of the Caledonian Railway in 1998, Class 86/2 No 86245 was painted by Willesden Depot into Caledonian blue offset by red stripes in the VT style, and also named* Caledonian. *It is seen outside Willesden following repaint.* **Author**

The AC Electrics

Left: *Painted in early InterCity 'Executive' livery, Class 86/4 No 86417* The Kingsman *climbs Shap incline at Greenholme on 17 July 1986 powering the 10.15 Euston–Carlisle service, formed of Mk2 stock and two Motorail vans coupled behind the locomotive.* **Author**

Right: *Taken at Bletchley on 29 August 1967, Class AL6 No E3167 is seen from its non-pantograph end sporting electric blue with a small yellow warning panel, complete with cast 'Lion holding Wheel' logo on the body side and cast numbers. This locomotive was renumbered to 86228 and named* Vulcan Heritage. **Author**

Left: *As part of British Rail's celebrations to mark the 150th anniversary of the Liverpool and Manchester Railway in 1979, the London Midland Region named No 86235* Novelty *after the original locomotive in the Rainhill trials. In addition to naming, the locomotive was given wrap-around yellow ends, large numbers and a Liverpool & Manchester logo on the side. It is seen looking rather grubby at Liverpool Lime Street in April 1980.* **Author**

Below: *Following privatisation and the Liverpool Street–Norwich InterCity route and Anglia branch lines being taken over by Anglia, the company house colours of turquoise were soon applied, a colour which many said was a mix of early electric blue and BR rail blue. TDM jumper-fitted No 86218* NHS 50 *is seen at Norwich and shows a couple of later modifications, a cab ventilator in the former route indicator panel, air guards covering the windscreen wipers and a single air compressor.* **Author**

Left: *Class 86s repainted for Rail express systems, which were later absorbed into EWS, were until the official merger, repainted in red and grey, a very pleasing colour scheme and one which suited the body profile of the class well. Parked in the works yard at Stratford Diesel Repair Shop on 13 July 1990, Class 86/4 No 86419* Poste Haste *displays these colours. This locomotive is fitted with both RCH and multi-pin control jumper systems, together with sealed beam marker lights and a high-intensity headlight.* **Author**

Left: *Following the take over of all three Trainload Freight companies as well as Rail express systems by US-owned English Welsh & Scottish Railway, the company's maroon and gold colour scheme was quickly applied to a representative selection of motive power. The first Class 86/2 to sport the livery was No 86261* The Rail Charter Partnership, *repainted in March 1997 and illustrated at Birmingham International on 20 March 1997 at the head of a passenger charter formed of TRCP stock.* **Author**

Class 87

Design: BR Workshops/English Electric Bo-Bo 25kV overhead AC electric
Number range: 87001-035, 87101
Introduced: 1973
Withdrawn: from 1999

Above: *Mostly in its original 'as built' condition, with the addition of its* Borderer *nameplate, No 87025 passes Willesden yard on 12 May 1980 powering a southbound express formed mainly of Mk2 stock. The locomotive at this time still had its original cross-arm pantograph; one change from its 'as delivered' condition is the repositioning of the double arrow logo from the middle of the body to under the non-driving cab side window.* **Author**

The fleet of Class 87s was ordered following authorisation for electrification of the London Midland/Scottish Region West Coast Main Line north from Weaver Junction to Glasgow. The existing fleets of AC electrics, dating from the 1950s/60s, would be insufficient for the new scheme. A fleet of 36 locomotives was ordered, classified 87, and numbered in the then standard TOPS 87xxx series.

Power and control equipment was supplied by GEC, with mechanical assembly carried out by British Rail Engineering Ltd (BREL) Crewe. The appearance of the class followed the previous AL1-AL6 designs, but on this BRB design only two front windscreens were used. Fixed-beam headlights and sealed beam marker/tail lights were installed as front indication, no provision was made for train reporting numbers.

A major departure from previous designs was the use of Flexicoil suspension and frame mounted traction motors.

The main body consisted of a fabricated underframe onto which the body was 'built'; the upper section and roof were removable to facilitate maintenance. As with previous designs both the body sides were of different style; one had an almost complete bank of air louvres, while the other was fitted with two glazed windows and four air grilles.

By the time the Class 87 fleet was ordered, the decision had been made to rid the network of vacuum-braked stock, and the '87s' were built from new with only train air brake equipment; initially this caused operational problems with locomotives assigned to trains fitted with vacuum brakes during the stock transition period.

The Class 87s were allocated to Willesden depot, where they remained throughout their life, except No 87101, which stayed at Crewe firstly for research operations and then for freight duties.

Power collection for the '87s' was originally by a single GEC cross-arm pantograph, but in the 1980s these were replaced by Brecknell Willis high speed pantographs allowing a top speed of 110mph.

When introduced in 1973/74 the class was painted in the then standard BR rail blue, with full yellow ends, which remaining until 1984 when various livery experiments were carried out, resulting in development of the main line and InterCity liveries of the 1990s. Various InterCity schemes were applied culminating in the InterCity 'Swallow' scheme. Following privatisation and the fleet passing to Virgin Trains, Virgin red and grey was applied to all operational members. This livery remained until the class was made redundant by Virgin following introduction of Pendolino and Voyager fixed formation trains. Soon after the Class 87 fleet was built, a BR locomotive naming policy was revived and the Class 87s became some of the first recipients.

The final locomotive of the build is worth special mention, originally allocated the number 87036, it was constructed by GEC/BR as a test-bed for the use of thyristors in traction control. Due to the many differences on the locomotive, it was decided to number it as a separate sub-class as 87101 to avoid confusion with conventional locomotives. After its release No 87101 was the subject of extensive testing to ascertain the benefits of the installation of modern electronics in traction systems. Much of the data obtained paved the way for the application of GEC thyristor control principles on the Class 90 and 91 fleets.

After its useful life was over as a development locomotive, it commenced operation for the Railfreight business and upon privatisation became the property of EWS, who retired it from use. It was sold in late 2001 and eventually broken up for scrap.

Above: *All 36 members of the Class 87 fleet were fabricated and built in the main erecting shop at BREL Crewe Works. The body shells were assembled in the main fabrication shop towards the south end of the complex and then transferred to the main assembly area where around six locomotives were under construction at the same time. The subject of this view is No 87004, with No 87005 close behind and No 87002 wheeled in the middle background.* **Author**

After the main fleet was made redundant by Virgin Trains, owner Porterbrook Leasing tried to find other work for the fleet. Suggestions were made of export deals with foreign operators, but by 2007 all but two of the fleet were still in the UK, the two exceptions being Nos 87012/019 working for operator BZK in Bulgaria. Three locomotives spent a short time operating for Carlisle-based operator Direct Rail Services, while a small

number operate for GB Railfreight and have been painted into house colours.

Very few structural alterations have taken place since this class was first introduced, the most noticeable being the installation of RCH style nose end jumpers used for TDM control, and the removal of the original multiple unit control boxes. The original quartz headlights were replaced with BR/Network Rail units of Group Standard design.

Below: *Now preserved at the National Railway Museum, York, No 87001* Royal Scot *passes Blackrigg, north of Carlisle, on 8 June 1979 powering the 07.45 Euston to Glasgow Central service. Under the revived naming policy, this locomotive was the first to be given a name when* Stephenson *was unveiled in a ceremony at London Euston on 14 January 1976, to mark the 150th anniversary of the Stockton & Darlington Railway. The name was put forward by the Stephenson Locomotive Society, who wanted the name to be applied to test-bed No 87101 but this was turned down. However, following agreement for fleet naming it was decided to make No 87001* Royal Scot *with the* Stephenson *plate being transferred to 87101. For some reason this locomotive has its running number applied in a lower position on the bodyside than normal.* **Author**

Above: In ex-works condition, No 87002 is seen just south of Crewe on the West Coast main line during a photo shoot on 7 July 1973, when less than a month into traffic. The locomotive is viewed from its pantograph end and clearly shows that the original painting scheme called for a half character space between the class number and running number. **Author**

Below: Sporting an early version of InterCity Executive livery, a very tatty No 87032 Kenilworth passes Clifton, south of Penrith, on 29 March 1990 forming the Cross-Country 15.15 Edinburgh–London Paddington. By the time this illustration was taken, No 87032 had gained TDM control cables on the nose end. **Author**

Above: *Sporting Executive livery, No 87023* Velocity *passes through Crewe station on the up fast track on 7 January 1992 leading a Mk2 formation on the 12.10 Liverpool Lime Street to Euston. This illustration was taken in the transition period of loco-hauled workings and fixed formation trains with Driving Van Trailers (DVTs) coupled at the London end. DVT No 82122 is seen on the left.* **Author**

Below: *Carrying InterCity Swallow livery, no multiple control jumpers but just an RCH connection, No 87026* Sir Richard Arkwright *stands at Glasgow Central station with overnight sleeper stock after arrival of the 23.55 service from London Euston on 3 June 2006.* **Author**

Above: *Following the completion of complex static and dynamic tests with Class 87/1 No 87101, which had the ability to be operated in both conventional or advanced modes, the locomotive was allocated to the freight sector and usually operated from Crewe. Under the sectorisation of the freight businesses prior to privatisation, it was allocated to Railfreight Speedlink/Distribution and repainted in triple grey livery with the two red diamond sign on the bodyside. The locomotive is seen inside Crewe Electric Depot in company with Class 86/6 No 86602 on 10 March 1993.* **Author**

Left: *Painted in standard Virgin Trains red livery, and with its nameplate towards the No 1 end, No 87024 Lord of the Isles pulls into Wolverhampton on 5 March 2001 forming the 11.15 service from London Euston. Once a full 'push-pull' railway was established on the West Coast Main Line, the locomotives were usually marshalled at the north end of formations and the DVT at the London end.* **Author**

The AC Electrics

Above: *Viewed from its walkway side, nameless No 87013 arrives at Glasgow Central on 12 August 1999 leading the 09.35 service from London Euston. This locomotive was originally named* John O'Gaunt *on 15 March 1978 with the plates removed in July 1998 when it was repainted in Virgin red.* **Author**

Below: *During the final years and months of Virgin Trains loco-hauled operations on both the CrossCountry and West Coast franchises, some unusual and interesting liveries were authorised. Several Class 87s were repainted, including No 87002 which emerged in its owner Porterbrook Leasing's mauve and white, carrying a large Porterbrook 'swan's head' logo on both sides. On 29 July 2004, it is seen leading the 06.55 Euston–Manchester Piccadilly through Crewe station. This locomotive would be one of the last to be withdrawn in 2006.* **Author**

Above: *A perfect view for the modellers, a broadside elevation of the pioneer member of the Class, No 87001 at BREL Crewe Works before delivery. Its No 1 end is on the left and we are looking at the cab-cab walkway side incorporating two glazed windows.* **Author**

Left: *The sole member of the Class 87/1 sub-class No 87101 built by BR and English Electric for the furtherance of electric traction propulsion systems. Much of the thyristor technology tried on this locomotive was later adopted for the Class 90 fleet, which at one time was to be classified as 87/2. No 87101 is seen near Preston during trial running.* **Author**

Below: *Two Class 87s were repainted by Willesden into futuristic liveries in May 1984 when the 'executive' or 'main line' schemes were under development. No 87012 in early 'Executive' and 87006 in all-over dark grey stand outside Willesden DED on 11 May 1984 prior to being shown to the BRB and entering service.* **Author**

Above: *Carrying InterCity 'Swallow' livery but having yellow cab window surrounds, No 87035 Robert Burns, the last member numerically of the standard fleet awaits departure from Carlisle on 26 May 1989 bound for Glasgow.* **Author**

Right: *Coupled ahead of a DVT on a southbound working, indicating probable TDM defects, No 87011 The Black Prince leads DVT No 82124 with the 11.40 Glasgow—London Euston out of Carlisle on 18 February 1997.* **Author**

Below: *To mark the end of the Class 87s on normal services out of Euston, Virgin Trains and Alstom Traincare arranged a line up of celebrity Class 87s at Wembley depot on 28 June 2005 when Nos 87001, 87002, 87010, 87012 and 87019, all in different colours, were placed on display to the railway media.* **Brian Morrison**

Class 89

Design: BREL/Brush Traction Co-Co 25kV overhead AC electric
Number range: 89001
Introduced: 1986
Withdrawn: from 1992

Above: *People either loved or hated the structural design of the BREL/Brush Class 89. Its design was certainly futuristic and pleasing to the eye, but its raked back inner end when coupled to passenger stock gave a weird visual effect. Painted in early InterCity livery, No 89001 is seen in company with Class 90 No 90008 and Class 91 No 91003 at the Engineering Development Unit, Derby on 19 May 1988 being prepared for shipment to Germany to take part in a rail exhibition in Hamburg.* **Author**

The first 25kV AC electric locomotive to emerge to a totally different basic body design to the original modernisation fleets was the BR/BREL/Brush prototype Class 89. Just one locomotive, No 89001, was built at BREL Crewe between 1984-87, BREL acting as sub-contractor to builder Brush Traction. Ordered in 1983, the locomotive incorporated very advanced traction equipment supplied by Brush Traction of Loughborough.

The structural design was a complete change to previous 25kV types, using a Co-Co wheel arrangement and incorporating streamlined cab ends, more reminiscent of the prototype Class 41 HSDT power cars.

No 89001 was built as a 'production' demonstrator with a rating of 5,850hp, which at the time, made it the most powerful electric locomotive in the UK. While its design was primarily for the high speed passenger operation, the locomotive had excellent operating characteristics for freight service.

Using a six-axle Co-Co bogie arrangement this provided 50 per cent better tractive effort than a Bo-Bo design. This level of tractive effort would have eliminated the need for double-heading many freight services over arduous inclines; however, BR engineers still favoured the Bo-Bo configuration, mainly for dynamic track force reasons.

After assembly No 89001 was transferred to Derby, and then by road to Brush Traction for exhaustive static electrical tests. After return to BR, No 89001 went back to BREL Crewe for several (minor) modifications to be made. By mid-1987 the locomotive was transferred to the Engineering Development Unit (EDU) at The Railway Technical Centre, Derby where pantograph, electrical and

structural tests were carried out, as well as 'type test' approval. These later tests were performed on the Old Dalby test track. As the line was not electrified at the time, traction was provided by a Class 47 propelling the locomotive and test coaches to evaluate high speed running. After acceptance by BR, the loco was first allocated to Crewe, from where tests over Shap incline and to Willesden, were conducted. Performance of the locomotive soon proved to be highly successful.

Much of the active testing was carried out powering the then new BR International Train and by October 1987 No 89001 had clocked up some 10,000 miles. However and very sadly, due to gauge restrictions the Class 89 was not permitted to enter Euston station so the locomotive never had the chance to power passenger services on the former LM route.

From the end of 1987 No 89001 was transferred to the East Coast Main Line (ECML) and allocated to Hornsey Depot and later transferred to Bounds Green, where driver training was conducted. The locomotive was used on the ECML until May 1988, following the delivery of the first Class 91. In late May it returned to the RTC Derby for preparation before being sent, together with a Class 90 and 91, to Hamburg for exhibition purposes. Returning to the UK, No 89001 resumed ECML duties, then worked alongside the Class 91 fleet until 1990, when due to technical defects, the locomotive was taken out of service and stored at Bounds Green. No 89001 was withdrawn in July 1992, and technically 'preserved' at the Midland Railway Centre, Butterley.

Railway privatisation in the UK could not envisage such a valuable asset lying in a preservation centre, and initiatives by its owners at

Butterley, eventually led to ECML operator Great North Eastern Railway purchasing the locomotive from the preservationists. After spending a period back at Brush Traction, where much new and updated equipment was fitted, No 89001 was repainted in GNER blue and orange livery and returned to traffic at Bounds Green.

To save the need for all ECML drivers to have to be trained on the unique locomotive, it was agreed that it would operate only on the King's Cross–Leeds/Bradford route. Sadly after a relatively short period, No 89001 was again in technical trouble with bogie traction faults which required it to be returned to the Brush Works for much of late 1999 and well into 2000. It returned to service in late 2000 only to have further problems. At the time GNER said it was their intention to return 89001 to front line service, but this never happened. It was eventually withdrawn and again entered 'preserved' status, now in the hands of The AC Locomotive Group at Barrow Hill.

The cab layout of the Class 89 was totally different from any other locomotive design, with a deep wrap-round desk incorporating easy-to see dials, and thoughtfully positioned controls. A novel feature (at the time) included on the Class 89 was a speed selector switch, whereby the driver could 'preselect' a required road speed, open the power controller to the full position and the locomotive's electronics would do the rest, regulating the speed to the required figure. This feature worked in both acceleration and deceleration modes. Speed selection equipment was subsequently installed on both the Class 90 and 91 fleets.

No 89001 was fitted with conventional Electric Train Supply (ETS) equipment, buck-eye couplers (the first time on an AC locomotive), and air and rheostatic (loco) braking. When completed, No 89001 was finished in original InterCity livery, this was later amended to the InterCity 'Swallow' scheme. On 16 January 1989 No 89001 was named *Avocet* after the Royal Society for the Protection of Birds, by the then Prime Minister Margaret Thatcher.

Right: *An early artist's impression of the proposed Class 89, produced by Brush some two years prior to the locomotive being built. The front end. while very similar to the finished product except that the position of the tail and headlights have changed positions, looks stunning with this front end livery treatment. It is interesting to see the representation of the pantograph looking more like a bow collector.* **Author's collection**

Below: *On 18 April 1985, the steel shell of the Class 89 was captured inside the pre-paint shop at BREL Crewe. Most of the steelwork was complete including the two equipment room bulkheads. After this view was taken the loco frame was clad with medium gauge steel and the cab ends applied before being taken into the main erecting shop.* **Author**

Above: *The Class 89 was deployed on the East Coast Main Line in the transition period between a diesel and electric railway, operating such trains as this 07.18 Peterborough–King's Cross commuter train on 30 August 1988, formed of a Mk3 HST set with a buffer-fitted DVT-modified Class 43 power car coupled behind the locomotive to act as a coupling adaptor for the stock. The train is seen passing Arlesey.* **Brian Morrison**

Below: *Much of the early testing of the Class 89 on the West Coast, carried out to obtain 'Type Test Approval' certification was done coupled to the then new 'BREL International Train'; sadly, due to gauge clearance this set was never allowed to use Euston station in London. On 7 May 1987 one of these test runs is seen passing Madeley near Crewe while returning north from Willesden.* **J Winkle**

Above: *A regular duty for No 89001, painted in full InterCity 'Swallow' livery was the 17.36 King's Cross–Peterborough commuter service in 1988-89. On a very wet 17 February 1989, No 89001 sits awaiting departure with a Mk2 IC rake, while from left to right HST power cars Nos 43197, 43074 and 43121 make ready to depart.*
Author

Right: *Emerging from the dark of Copenhagen Tunnel between King's Cross and Finsbury Park, the unique Class 89 carrying InterCity 'Swallow' livery heads north on the ECML with a charter formed of the BR Special Trains unit's Mk1 stock on 27 May 1990.*
Brian Morrison

Above: *With all the technical problems encountered with No 89001 working passenger traffic for GNER, mainly attributable to the locomotive being a 'one off' and a shortage of spare parts, it is surprising that it survived in traffic for as long as it did. On 10 June 1999, No 89001 is seen painted in GNER blue with white GNER decals at Leeds after arrival of the 09.05 service from London King's Cross. On the left Virgin CrossCountry powercar No 43197 forms a northbound service to York.* **Author**

Below: *Painted in GNER livery, No 89001 passes South Elmsall between Doncaster and Wakefield Westgate on 16 July 1997 powering the 15.40 London King's Cross–Bradford Forster Square service.* **Russell Ayre**

Above: *Displaying InterCity 'Swallow' livery, complete with its* Avocet *nameplate and RSPB logo above, No 89001 is seen from its No 1 end. The front end in this livery style looked a little cluttered, with the glazed recessed light groups and black ventilation grilles. Since original assembly, a cab-to-shore radio telephone was added, this required an aerial located on the cab roof centrally above the front screen.* **Author**

Below: *On 16 November 1999, carrying full GNER livery with gold GNER branding, No 89001 is seen on works stands inside the main erecting shop at Brush Traction, Loughborough sharing workshop space with a DRS Class 37 and a Freightliner Class 47.* **Author**

Class 90

Design: BR/BREL/GEC Bo-Bo 25kV overhead AC electric
Number range: 90001-150
Introduced: 1987
Withdrawn: Still active

Above: *This was the first public view of what was to become the Class 90. When this illustration was taken at BREL Crewe on 4 July 1987, the official classification was Class 87/2 and this locomotive was identified as No 87201. Although looking near complete, the locomotive was far from finished. The front end was just a solid GRP moulding, while standard oval buffers were fitted and no buck-eye coupling attached. The livery was, however, 'marked out' for an application of InterCity paint.* **Author**

During the mid-1980s British Railways sought new-generation AC electric locomotives for WCML use, and financial authorisation was requested from the Government for a fleet of 50 thyristor-controlled state-of-the-art machines in 1984. Permission for the build was granted, and the BRB awarded construction to BREL who gave the assembly work to Crewe Works. The main equipment sub-contractor was GEC Traction.

At the time of the order, and indeed on early artists impressions, the locomotives were to be classified 87/2, being viewed at the time as very much a follow on from the 1970s Class 87 build. However as the assembly of the first locomotive neared completion, the new order was given the classification of 90.

This design was however a major change from previous 25kV AC designs in both structural and equipment configuration. The body incorporated steeply raked ends, and for the first time on a production loco, Time Division Multiplex (TDM) control equipment was installed.

Assembly at BREL Crewe started in late 1986, with the first locomotive shown to the public at the July 1987 open day; it was not, however, finished until September. After completion at Crewe, No 90001 was transferred to the Engineering Development Unit at the Railway Technical Centre, Derby, for 'type test' approval and commissioning. Delivery of the 50 locomotives was a drawn-out affair, with the final machine not handed over to the BRB until the end of 1990.

The Class 90s were designed for mixed traffic (passenger and freight) operation, with specific batches allocated to different work operations. The first batch were allocated to the passenger InterCity business, and once tests had been completed and sufficient stock fitted with TDM interface equipment, together with Driving Van Trailers (DVTs) introduced, the locomotives commenced operation on Euston to Birmingham, Manchester, Liverpool and Glasgow routes, working in push-pull mode, and taking over from Class 81-85 on front-line services.

Subsequent Class 90s were constructed for the then Railfreight Distribution (RfD) business for deployment on high-speed long-distance freight services. By 1992 the allocation of the class had been slightly amended with a small number dedicated to operating mail and postal services under the Rail express systems (Res) banner.

After splitting of the railway into businesses prior to mid-1990s privatisation, most of the Class 90s funded by Railfreight were reclassified to Class 90/1, which identified the isolation of their electric train supply (ETS) equipment. Renumbering was made in the 901xx series. This change left InterCity Class 90s as Nos 90001-90015 allocated to Willesden for passenger work, with the remainder, Nos 90016-025 and 90126-150 shedded at Crewe for freight work. In the immediate pre-privatisation period, the freight locomotives were again split, with Nos 90016-039 allocated to Railfreight and

Nos 90140-150 to Freightliner, with 90126-39 regaining their original numbers.

Under the big sell-off, Railfreight's locomotives became the property of EWS and those with Freightliner passed to the Freightliner company. The passenger locomotives passed to Porterbrook Leasing.

Some further renumbering was then carried out to return the EWS locos to the 900xx series, and in 2001 this was further amended with 110mph EWS locos with increased brake force classified as 90/2.

In 1990, when the East Coast Main Line (ECML) was fully electrified, the Class 90s started to appear on some duties from King's Cross, mainly deputising for Class 91s and for a short time from winter 1991 the class was rostered on ECML services. The Res-owned locomotives also started to operate over the electrified ECML on Royal Mail and van workings.

Freightliner's locomotives have a wide operating range, covering the entire WCML through London and into Essex on container traffic.

With the replacement of loco-hauled trains on Virgin Trains West Coast Main Line by 2002/03 the fleet was displaced by Pendolino stock. The 15 passenger members were then re-hired to the operators of the Anglia main line between London Liverpool Street and Norwich, now operated by 'one' Railway. Here the fleet displaced Class 86s.

A major feature of the Class 90s from new was the installation of drop-head buck-eye couplers with retractable side buffers - a feature deemed essential for high-speed passenger push-pull operation. Although all locomotives were built with this feature, those which became operated by the freight businesses had the equipment removed and many operated by Freightliner also had the electric train supply equipment isolated.

The livery applied to the first 25 Class 90s, when built, was full InterCity, with the next 11 emerging in Main Line livery, the final 14 were painted in RfD colours. Following the introduction of the Res red livery, the five locomotives operated by this business were repainted into the house colours. After privatisation, the 15 passenger locomotives were repainted in Virgin red and more recently in 'one' Railway turquoise, EWS locomotives either carry RfD triple grey, EWS maroon or Res red, while Freightliner locomotives are either in grey with Freightliner branding or carry Freightliner green and yellow.

Several 'one-off' or special liveries have been carried by the fleet, including French, Belgian and German railway colours, GNER blue/red and more recently First ScotRail colours for powering the overnight sleeper services between London Euston and Edinburgh/Glasgow.

Right: *This view of the BREL Crewe Works production line taken on 13 February 1988 shows Nos 90007 and 90008 for use by the InterCity passenger business taking shape. It will be noted that compared with the illustration on the previous page a number of changes to the GRP cab front section had been made; also trimmed rotating retractable buffers and a space for the drop-head coupler was provided. The assembly of the Class 90s was a drawn-out affair with some locomotives taking 12 months from sheet steel to a complete operational locomotive; this should be viewed in comparison with the General Electric production line in the USA where the average total build time is less than three weeks.* **Author**

Below: *Although a locomotive which was later taken over by the Rail express system arm and then by EWS, No 90019 shows the 'as delivered' InterCity 'Swallow' livery. This locomotive is seen at Carlisle at the head of a southbound charter on 6 September 1991. Note that its buck-eye coupler is in the raised position and that the buffers are retracted.* **Author**

Above: *Originally the receptacle for the nose end RCH cables was in two clips in the recessed section of the front bodywork below the horn grille. However, this was not well accepted by staff and a revised stowage point on the side of the buffer shank was provided. With central clips present but not in use, No 90004 passes Carpenders Park on 19 November 1990 powering a Manchester–Euston express. At this time the train should have been driven from the DVT, but TDM configuration problems led to the train being loco-hauled.* **Author**

Below: *With the RCH jumpers housed in their intended position, No 90003 is seen under the great roof at Glasgow Central station on 24 January 1990 powering a rake of Mk2 stock to Polmadie depot after arriving with a CrossCountry service from Plymouth. On the left is a Class 303 electric multiple unit awaiting to form a service to Motherwell.* **Author**

Above: *On a very wet 23 March 1994, InterCity 'Swallow' liveried No 90010 275 Railway Squadron (Volunteers) arrives at Glasgow Central with empty Mk3 stock from Polmadie depot to form the 09.50 to London Euston. In full IC 'Swallow' livery and coupled to a set of Mk3s, the Class 90s probably looked their best.* **Author**

Right: *During driver training of Anglia main line staff on Class 90s, Main Line-liveried No 90028 approaches Colchester on 5 April 1990 heading a 14.00 Ipswich—Ilford training special formed of Railfreight coal hoppers.* **Author**

Below: *Sporting the Main Line version of the InterCity colours, No 90031 makes light work of Shap incline at Greenholme on 30 March 1990 powering the 09.45 Euston—Carlisle formed of Mk3 stock with two Motorail vans coupled behind the locomotive.* **Author**

Above: *Following the formation of the Class 90/1 sub-class and their dedication to Railfreight traffic, a number of repaints were undertaken. Showing the replacement of the original retractable buffers with standard oval units and the removal of the drop-head coupler, No 90126, in full Railfreight Distribution livery, stands inside Crewe Electric Depot on 10 March 1993 following naming after the depot.* **Author**

Below: *Another view taken inside Crewe Electric depot, showing some interesting front end modifications. On the left is No 90018, dedicated to the Rail express systems business, retaining drop-head buck couplers and retractable buffers, while No 90136 on the right has blanking plates inserted over the original position of the Pullman rubbing plate, has only a screw coupling but retained original buffers, which were presumably 'locked' in the extended position.* **Author**

Above: *Painted in Railfreight Distribution livery, complete with a Crewe Depot 'eagle' logo on the cab side, No 90133 hurries past Atherton on the southbound fast track on 20 March 1997 powering the 12.08 Halewood to Wembley Yard export automotive train.* **Author**

Below: *When Freightliner commenced operation as a private company, their locos were mainly painted in the BR triple grey colour scheme, as at the time no new livery had been devised and Freightliner branding was applied to the grey bodywork. Here No 90049 drops down Beattock Bank near Abington on 6 April 2006 powering the 08.02 Crewe Basford Hall to Glasgow Coatbridge container service. This locomotive has lost its buck-eye coupler, Pullman rubbing plate and cast Crewe depot logo from the cab side nearest the camera.* **Chris Perkins**

Above: *For the events surrounding the commencement of the Virgin Trains West Coast franchise on 10 March 1997, Class 90/0 No 90002 was repainted into Virgin Trains red livery and renamed* Mission Impossible, *reflecting on the challenge ahead for Virgin Trains to revolutionise rail travel on the west coast route. No 90002 is seen at Manchester Piccadilly after forming the first VT 'red' service on the west Coast, a press and VIP special from London Euston.* **Author**

Middle: *During the period of passenger loco-hauled operation on the West Coast route since privatisation, Willesden depot held the responsibility for around 90 per cent of maintenance work, which during the later years with a shortage of spare parts and a run-down fleet was not always an easy challenge. On 27 March 2001, No 90014 is seen inside the depot. This was the only locomotive to carry the Virgin Trains 'lady' logo on the cab side. Depot space is being shared with various Class 86/2s and 87024.* **Author**

Left: *Over the years the Class 90 fleet has carried a wide selection of names, some reflecting the line of route, others people, some advertising other customers and depots associated with the fleet. On 6 April 1993, InterCity named No 90002* The Girls' Brigade *in a ceremony at London Euston, when HM The Queen Mother unveiled the cast plate complete with cast logo above. The plates remained on the locomotive until February 1997 when they were removed, as No 90002 was the chosen locomotive for the launch of the Virgin Trains franchise as shown above.* **Author**

Above: *After transfer from Virgin Trains to 'one' railway, the 15 passenger locomotives have been progressively repainted into the attractive 'one' Railway turquoise colour scheme. In this livery, No 90013 approaches Colchester on 8 September 2006 powering the 13.00 Norwich—London Liverpool Street service. The deployment of spare Mk3 stock and Class 90s on to the Liverpool Street-Norwich route has improved route performance and passenger comfort.* **Author**

Below: *In 2004, Freightliner started to repaint its Class 90/0s in house colours of green and yellow, which looks very distinctive and suits the body profile well. Here No 90041 is seen stabled between duties at Ipswich station on 14 October 2004. The Freightliner Class 90 fleet operates mainly on the Scotland/North West to East Anglia intermodal corridor.* **Brian Morrison**

Above: *Standard British Railways InterCity livery as applied originally to the first 25 locomotives, destined for front line passenger operations. No 90010 Penny Black, a locomotive later taken over by Rail express systems for Royal Mail and charter traffic, is seen at Carlisle from its No 1 end on 6 September 1991. In this scheme white cab roofs were applied with a yellow panel both above and below the headlight band.* **Author**

Below: *In association with FretConnection 1992, a freight exhibition held in London, three members of the Class 90 freight fleet were repainted into European operators' liveries; No 90129 in DB (German Railways) red, No 90128 in SNCB (Belgian Railways) blue, and No 90130 in SNCF (French Railways) colours. Together with No 90022 in Railfreight livery, they are seen at Trafford Park on 5 October 1993 taking part in the FretConnection event of that year which was held in Manchester.* **Author**

Above: *Perhaps too bright for some railway followers, Virgin red and grey always looked smart on a clean locomotive. The livery style for Virgin Trains, based on the company's red profile, was supplemented by three white longitudinal bands and the simple 'Virgin' name behind the cab door at each end. Running numbers were applied in white, with no repeat of the last three digits on the front end. No 90002* Mission Impossible *is shown outside Willesden depot on 13 February 1998.* **Author**

Below: *After the transfer of the 15 Porterbrook-owned passenger locomotives to 'one' Railway based in Norwich, the Class 90/0s started to emerge in company house colours. In immaculate condition, No 90007* Sir John Betjeman *passes Colchester on 8 September 2006 returning light loco to Norwich following naming at London Liverpool Street.* **Author**

Class 91

Design: BR/BREL/GEC Bo-Bo 25kV overhead AC electric
Number range: 91001-031, 91101-132
Introduced: 1988
Withdrawn: Still active

Above: *The official roll-out for the first Class 91 was held at BREL Crewe on 14 February 1988 and attended by a large number of railway officials, VIPs and members of the railway press. No 91001 was one of the first locomotives to sport the full InterCity 'Swallow' livery scheme. For the event the locomotive, which only carried numbers on the lower body at the 'blunt' end, was given GEC branding on its buffer.* **Author**

By 1984, when the Advanced Passenger Train (APT) project was all but over, the design and deployment of new locomotives and stock for the WCML were of prime importance. This led to the InterCity 225 project emerging, which considered construction of APT-style driving power cars hauling trailer passenger vehicles and a fleet of Driving Van Trailers (DVTs) for coupling at the remote end of train formations.

The main engineering groups were invited to pre-qualify for a bid to build 25 train sets in Autumn 1984. At the time the BR guidelines stipulated a requirement that the 'loco' must have the ability also to power lower-speed sleeper or freight trains by night.

In the autumn of 1984 came the authorisation for East Coast Main Line (ECML) electrification; originally the Class 89 Co-Co design (then under development) was the preferred choice for this route, but soon, the BR InterCity team decided to steer further development towards the IC225 principle for both East and West Coast routes. By early 1985 an IC225 development team was formed for the ECML project. In April 1985, under the BRB competitive tendering process, three firms were invited to submit building tenders for the project; these were ASEA of Sweden, Brush Traction and GEC Transportation projects (GEC-TPL). After much deliberation the contract was placed with GEC in February 1986.

GEC was given the complete design, build and test remit, although as in previous electric locomotive orders, the main contractor GEC sub-contracted mechanical construction to BREL who awarded the work to its Crewe site.

Under BR's numerical classification the locomotives became Class 91 and the stock was later identified as Mk4.

Following contract agreement in February 1986 it was announced that the first locomotive would roll out on 14 February 1988. Following this announcement, design and construction went full speed ahead, and despite many problems encountered, the roll-out was met. Many novel features were incorporated in the fleet, including a streamlined or 'raked' No 1 end for high speed running, and a slab-fronted No 2 end for slower speed work. One of the most significant changes was in bogie and traction design, incorporating frame mounted traction motors driving an axle-mounted gearbox via a carden shaft. The disc brake unit was 'off wheel' and fitted on the rear of the traction motor. The Class 91 also incorporated the latest state-of-the-art computer-based electronics for power and brake control.

In common with all new high-speed locomotives, buck-eye auto couplers were fitted, and a Time Division Multiplex (TDM) system installed for remote control from DVT stock.

After the GEC/BREL roll out at Crewe, No 91001 commenced type test approval, first from Crewe and then at the Engineering Development Unit, at the Railway Technical Centre, Derby. By March 1988, No 91001 was delivered to its new home at Bounds Green for ECML testing and training.

Due to protracted deliveries of the purpose built-Mk4 DVT vehicles, several HST power cars were adapted for TDM operation, and a limited passenger service powered by Class 91s commenced in

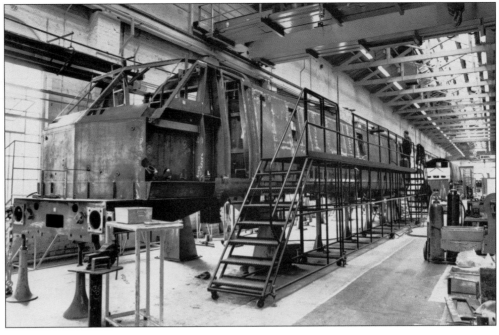

Right: *The penultimate Class 91, No 91030 is seen in the main fabrication shop at BREL Crewe on 4 September 1990, in the background is the more advanced shell of No 91028. The assembly of the Class 91s was a drawn out affair, not only with 10 being built first and then the balance of 21, but also the timescale of each locomotive under the assembly process, with on average 30 weeks from sheet steel to complete locomotive.* **Author**

October 1989. Full use of Class 91s started in 1992.

The original delivery order for Class 91s was for just 10 locomotives; these were introduced for evaluation running, and after thousands of running hours, the manufacturers then commenced construction of the remaining 21 to make a fleet size of 31 locomotives. The final example was completed in February 1991.

The Class 91s have always operated on the East Coast electrified route, working all non-HST duties on the King's Cross–Leeds, Newcastle, Edinburgh and Glasgow route. After privatisation the fleet was transferred to HSBC Rail and remained hired to the East Coast operator Great North Eastern Railway, their dark blue and red house colours replacing the original InterCity 'Swallow' livery.

Under InterCity ownership, most locomotives were named,

a policy eventually continued by GNER.

From 2000 a major refurbishment of the Class 91 fleet commenced at Adtranz Doncaster, with attention to internal equipment by Alstom. The work comprised a major package of reliability modifications, plus the re-design of the No 1 cab. Modified locomotives were reclassified in the Class 91/1 sub-class, retaining the last two digits of their original number.

One interesting development in Class 91 history came in October 2000 and February 2001, when the same Class 91 was involved in accidents at Hatfield and Great Heck; in both cases the locomotive was not the primary cause and was returned to service. However, after the second incident it was agreed to renumber the locomotive upon refurbishing, from 91023 to 91132.

Below: *By the end of 1988 most of the first ten Class 91s were undergoing either static or dynamic testing or in use for staff training. The deployment of electric traction on the East Coast main line was a major undertaking, with every member of existing train crew having a conversion course from diesel to electric traction, being taught overhead electrification safety and being brought up to speed on new handling techniques. On 28 November 1988, No 91008 awaits departure from King's Cross bound for Peterborough with a Mk3 formed training special.* **Author**

Above: *Negotiating the old Leeds City electrified layout on 14 January 1991, No 91004 approaches the station with the 12.10 service from King's Cross. Under usual operation on the East Coast route, the Class 91s were coupled to the north end of trains, with a Mk4 DVT at the south or London end.* **Author**

Below: *Probably one of the most spectacular stations in the world for photography is York, located on a tight curve and with a wonderful, well kept dual-ended train shed. On the northbound main platform line on 21 January 1993, No 91023 leads the 11.00 King's Cross–Glasgow Central service. If compared with the first picture of this section, this locomotive shows the InterCity 'Swallow' livery with standard number position.* **Author**

Above: *There are very few occasions that pairs of Class 91s have been recorded on one train, usually only in the very rare case of failure, but then assistance is usually provided by a diesel, or where locomotives are being transferred between depots for maintenance. On 10 March 1989, while training and testing of the first 10 locomotives was being undertaken, Nos 91003 and 91006 pose on the front of a training run in Doncaster West Yard.* **Author**

Below: *Complete with cast silver swallow logo on the front, a very short lived fitting, No 91025 passing Harringay on 7 December 1993 forming the 14.10 King's Cross–Leeds service. Although deemed as fixed consist trains, the Class 91 and Mk4 sets usually operate with the leading end buck-eye coupling in the lowered or normal position, ready for the attachment of conventional coupling stock.* **Author**

Above: *Just before refurbishment to a Class 91/1, No 91028 departs from Edinburgh Waverley on 25 October 2001 leading the 06.15 Doncaster to Glasgow Central service. Compared to the original bright InterCity 'Swallow' livery, the GNER dark blue offset by a red/orange band looked very drab; however, in good light a clean all-blue set does look impressive on the main line at full speed.* **Author**

Middle: *With only 31 class members and the large number of trains operated each day by GNER, very little spare capacity in diagrams exists and the sight of a light or spare Class 91 is rare. Sometimes changeovers of locomotivess take place at King's Cross, especially if problems are reported by an incoming train. On 28 May 1998 No 91023, complete with early white GNER branding, is seen slab end first at King's Cross.* **Author**

Left: *As part of the HSBC refurbishment contract, the driving cab at the leading end was heavily rebuilt to incorporate new equipment including Drivers Vigilance Device and TPWS. The work improved the driver's environment and was welcomed by the staff. The cab of No 91127 (renumbered from No 91027), the first locomotive to be refurbished, is seen at King's Cross on 16 January 2001.* **Author**

Above: *In fully refurbished state, No 91111* Terence Cuneo *passes track-relaying work at Drem Loops on 30 September 2005 while leading the 07.00 King's Cross to Glasgow Central service. In their original guise under BR the Class 91s carried cast nameplates, sadly under GNER 'stick-on' names have been used.* **Chris Perkins**

Below: *Led by No 91130* City of Newcastle, *the 07.00 King's Cross—Glasgow Central crosses Slateford Viaduct on the exit from Edinburgh Waverley on 28 February 2005. The reliability of the Class 91s is good, but GNER employ four 'Thunderbird' Class 67 diesel locomotives to rescue trains in case of failure or infrastructure problems, which require services to operate away from the electrified area.* **Chris Perkins**

Above: *Showing the original InterCity 'Swallow' livery, with small numbers applied only at the inner end, No 91003 stands with Class 90 No 90008 and Class 89 No 89001 at the Railway Technical Centre, Derby on 19 May 1988. All three were en route to Hamburg for display of the very latest European traction.* **Author**

Left: *In mid-green body primer, the body shell of No 91028 is seen in the main erecting shop at BREL Crewe on 4 September 1990. At this stage in construction most of the technical equipment was fitted and the glass reinforced plastic front flat end was awaited. Note that the glazed windows are protected in preparation for a visit to the paint shop.* **Author**

Above: *In line with BR's policy to name its main-line traction, No 91003 was given the name* The Scotsman *to mark the 175th anniversary of the newspaper. The cast plate also incorporated the masthead logo of the paper. The unveiling was carried out by the paper's then Editor, Magnus Linklater, in a ceremony at Edinburgh Waverley station on 25 February 1993. Still in pristine condition on 25 June 1996, the locomotive hurries through Doncaster powering the 07.50 King's Cross-Leeds express.* **Author**

Below: *Displaying the 'Privatised' GNER livery of dark blue and red/orange, complete with gold bodyside decals, No 91107* Newark-on-Trent, *with a full rake of Mk4s and DVT No 82218 on the rear, heads the 06.15 King's Cross to Edinburgh Waverley along the Prestonpans divergence at Dolphingstone on 4 April 2006.* **Chris Perkins**

Class 92

Design: BR/Brush Co-Co 25kV AC overhead/750V DC third rail dual power electric
Number range: 92001-046
Introduced: 1993
Withdrawn: Still active

Above: *To allow deliveries to run concurrent to all three Class 92 operators, no strict numeric sequence was followed for each batch with various members being 'allocated' as the build progressed. French Railways SNCF-owned No 92006* Louis Armand, *complete with SNCF branding is seen outside North Pole depot in West London during early testing.* **Author**

The Class 92s which emerged in the early 1990s for Cross-Channel freight and passenger use are some of the most technically complex locomotives in the world. The fleet emerged from a design project in May 1988 when various traction alternatives were considered for powering Cross-Channel freight and overnight passenger trains through the Channel Tunnel.

A number of design/build consortia from both the UK and Mainland Europe put design options forward, but the one which was eventually accepted came from Brush Traction of Loughborough UK.

At the design stage it was obvious that these locomotives would not only have to meet the present UK operating 'Group Standards' but also satisfy the Channel Tunnel authorities and if, as was originally proposed, to use the fleet over European administrations, the design would have to meet full UIC specification.

The original order for Class 92s was placed on 22 July 1990 for 20 locomotives, followed by three smaller 'follow-on' orders for 10, seven and nine locomotives giving a fleet size of 46. Of these 'follow-on' options nine locomotives were funded by the French national rail operator SNCF and seven by the then European Passenger Services division of Eurostar.

The heavy Co-Co supported Class 92 body structure was broadly based on the previous Brush Class 60 diesel, but many major structural advances, especially in the front end area, had to be made to meet Eurotunnel and European railway safety requirements. After the design was agreed serious concern was levelled by the European railway trade unions over the crashworthiness of the design, and in

reality the design has never been authorised to operate further than a mile or two into France to exchange traction with French power.

In common with Brush Traction's usual policy, the Class 92 body shells were sourced from outside industry, being assembled by Procor of Wakefield. The body shells were formed of an underframe onto which side sections and cab ends were added, all pre-painted prior to road transfer to Loughborough.

Such was the requirement for safety when operating through the Channel Tunnel, the Class 92s had to be designed as virtually two locomotives within one shell, with all equipment duplicated to ensure that any *en route* failure would not stop a train from proceeding.

Construction at Loughborough was started in 1992 with the first locomotive complete at the end of 1993 and tested on site. It was handed over to BR Railfreight in February 1994. Delivery of the balance was a protracted affair, with the final loco not being delivered until 1996. Although owned by BR Railfreight, SNCF and EPS, all locos were operated at the time in a joint pool based at Crewe Electric Depot.

Such was the complexity of the on-board electronic and control systems, entry into traffic and certification by Railtrack (Network Rail) took a long time, the first route to use the fleet was through the Channel Tunnel between Dollands Moor and Calais Frethun, in the end agreement and certification was granted for the fleet to operate between North London and the Channel Tunnel, this was followed by the northern sections of the West Coast Main Line and by the northern sections of the East Coast Main Line and the entire West Coast route.

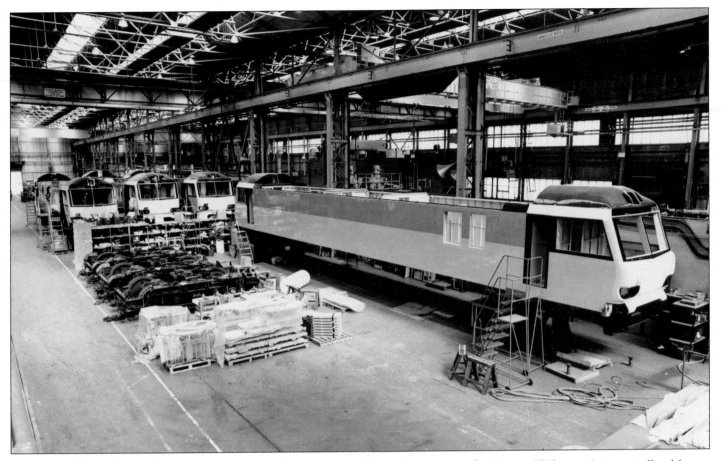

The locomotives are equipped to operate from either a 25kV AC overhead or at reduced traction output from the former Southern Region 750V DC third rail supply.

Signalling and control systems allow interface with Eurotunnel and SNCF systems. However, operation in France is restricted to the terminal at Calais, this being governed by the non-fitting of French cab signalling.

The locomotives funded by EPS (now Eurostar UK Ltd) were designed to power overnight 'Nightstar' services between the UK and France, but when this service was abandoned the locomotives became redundant and were operated by the UK privatised freight operator EWS, who became the owner of the original Railfreight locomotives. In 2000 the Eurostar UK locomotives were offered for sale and as no purchaser came forward the fleet became stored at Crewe. The French-owned locomotives were also stored and from 2006 efforts have been made by SNCF to restore the fleet to use and under an open access agreement operate freight services in the UK. A major development came in early 2007 when three locomotives were sold to Eurotunnel for use on cross-channel freight. In summer 2007 the locomotives are receiving refurbishment at Brush Traction, Loughborough.

All locos were built carrying the triple grey livery, with their owner's branding applied to the cab side. Two locomotives, Nos 92001/031, have since been repainted into full EWS maroon/gold livery.

Above: *The delivery of body shells from Procor at Horbury, Wakefield outstripped demand at the Loughborough factory and at times shells were stored at either the Procor factory or at Brush. Brush used 34 Shop to store shells and carry out some early assembly work. This view taken on 9 May 1992 shows No 92044 nearest the camera, with Nos 92043, 92042 and 92041 in the background viewed from left to right.* **Author**

Right: *With such a complex locomotive, considerable dynamic testing of the design was needed to gain a UK safety case and full type test approval. On 22 November 1994, before the class was authorised to take power from the National Network, a test run was carried out over Shap incline powered by Nos. 92003, 92018 and 92005 complete with various test cars and train make up vehicles. The actual test train illustrated was diesel hauled from Crewe to Carnforth by Class 47 No 47205, which was then attached to the rear of the train for its run to Carlisle in case of problems.* **Chris Dixon**

Above: *Working on the 25kV AC supply, No 92017* Shakespeare *is seen at Carlisle on 31 March 1995 during a period of fleet commissioning and staff training. As these locomotives were very different from previous AC classes, a major driver training and handling operation was undertaken, mainly using the northern section of the West Coast Main Line.* **Author**

Below: *Running on third-rail power supply, one of the early training and revenue earning trains to be powered by a Class 92 is seen passing Lenham on 30 July 1996 with the 09.37 Wembley to Lille. The Class 92 operated this train as far as Calais Frethun before returning to the UK.* **Author**

Above: *A rare view of a Class 92 actually operating in France, is this of No 92031, taking the spur off the International Main Line at Frethun into the SNCF marshalling yard on 13 July 1996, where a locomotive exchange took place. The train is the 09.33 Dagenham to Silla automotive parts train. At the time this locomotive was named* Schiler*, which was removed in 2006 when the locomotive was repainted into EWS red and gold livery and named* The Institute of Logistics and Transport. **Author**

Below: *In a view which is not recognisable today, following construction of the Channel Tunnel Rail Link (CTRL), No 92015 emerges from Saltwood Tunnel on 31 July 1996 leading a short international consist forming the 08.42 Somain to Wembley.* **Author**

Above: *An early view inside No 25 Shop at Brush Traction, Loughborough shows No 92002 on the left being fitted out and the bodyshell of No 92004 being lifted high by the two gantry cranes along the shop after arriving by road. On the right side of the shop Bo-Bo-Bo Eurotunnel 'Shuttle' locomotives Nos 9018 and 9017 take shape.* **Author**

Left: *Class 92 driving cab layout. Broadly based on that of the Class 60, the driver's power controller is on the right side on a separate pedestal, while the brake controllers are located on the left side. The screen on the left side of the main display panel is the main fault and control diagnostic panel. The cab from No 92003 is shown.* **Author**

Above: *In 'as delivered' BR livery, No 92009* Elgar *is seen at Willesden on 27 June 1994. During the livery design for this fleet, it was agreed to incorporate three 'tunnel segment' roundels on the body side; produced in polished aluminium; these are supposed to represent the Channel Tunnel.* **Author**

Below: *Running on 750V DC third rail power supply, No 92012 approaches Otford on 30 July 1996 powering the 13.45 Dollands Moor to Wembley formed of slide body cargo waggons. The loop track in the foreground was installed as part of the Channel Tunnel works to provide extra capacity for freight traffic through Kent.* **Author**

Electric Multiple-Units

It was the 1950s that saw the mass introduction of multiple-unit trains on the UK rail network; other than the London Underground, a few had been operated from the early years of the 20th century, but these were generally in highly populated areas, especially around London and the South East where mass transit was needed.

In terms of alternating current (AC) technology, as mentioned in the earlier sections of this book, the early users were the London Brighton & South Coast Railway and the Midland Railway on the Lancaster–Morecambe/Heysham routes. Although much was learned from the latter scheme, especially after 'modernisation' to industrial AC frequency in the 1950s, many of the mainstream projects of the period favoured direct current (DC) equipment, either collecting power from an overhead power line or a third rail supply.

It was really towards the end of the 1950s that AC units started to emerge for use on new electrification schemes on the London Midland and Scottish Regions, this was quickly followed by upgrading DC overhead systems on the Great Eastern routes from DC to AC supply. Apart from South Thames routes and in the Liverpool and Tyneside areas, no further DC electrification was then undertaken with all new schemes using overhead power collection AC supply.

Various designs of BTC/BR units emerged in the 1960s-1980s, but following privatisation in the 1990s the railway-owned workshops became a thing of the past and the private sector took over the refinement and design of modern multiple-unit EMUs, introducing state of the art, high speed complex traction units. However, sadly, in the main this has meant production has been transferred overseas,

to builders such as Siemens and Alstom. The former BR workshops largely became part of Bombardier Transportation and they still retain a major multiple-unit construction facility in Derby.

In years past multiple-unit trains were generally used for short to medium distance journeys with comfort levels tailored to match. However today, with huge refinements in design, ride quality and much improved ambience, the vast majority of new passenger trains in the UK and indeed throughout the world are based on the unit or multiple-unit philosophy. In the UK, the Pendolino train sets now plying the Virgin Trains west coast route from London to Glasgow, Wolverhampton, Liverpool and Manchester are very much unit or fixed train technology, capable of travelling at 125mph and fitted with tilt equipment.

In the main no standard design of EMU has ever been followed in the UK, with route or area specific stock being built; the nearest thing to a standard EMU came in the 1980s when BREL introduced its Class 321 range. Later from the workshops of ABB, then Bombardier came the 'Electrostar' family, a design which could easily be changed and amended for diesel or electric propulsion and offered in numerous different internal configurations from suburban to main line specification. Siemens, when they entered the UK train building arena, offered their 'Desiro' product range and again this was made available in diesel or electric configurations for virtually any type of area and route usage.

Over the next few pages we will look at the various designs of electric multiple-units, with details of their area of use, deployment and liveries.

Below: *Following conversion to industrial frequency AC supply, the Lancaster–Morecambe/Heysham line still operated at 6,600V, but now took its power supply from North Western Electricity Board. A three-car set with its driving trailer, No M29022M, nearest the camera, stands at Lancaster Green Ayre while route testing was in progress in the early part of 1953.* **Author's collection**

Above: Class AM6/Class 306. *Originally built as DC units for London Liverpool Street–Shenfield electrification in 1949, these three-car sets were later rebuilt for AC operation on the same route. Fitted with two-part sliding doors, the sets remained in traffic until the early 1980s. On 3 November 1980, set No 023 approaches Bethnal Green with a service to Gidea Park. The livery shown is standard BR rail blue.* **Author**

Below: Class AM4/Class 304. *Originally built for use on the Crewe–Manchester electrification, these sets followed the 1950s 'standard' design. This class was originally formed of 15 sets, but as electrification on the LM network spread, a further 30 units were built. Originally sets were designed to operate from both 6.25 and 25kV power supplied, but later all were converted to 25kV operation. No 032 is shown in BR green livery with small yellow warning panel.* **Author's collection**

Above: <u>Class AM4/Class 304.</u> *In common with most classes of UK multiple-unit train, many changes have taken place over the years, in terms of formation, interior layout and livery. Now reduced to a three-car formation (with its TS removed) set No 304009 stops at Heald Green on 30 April 1992 with a service from Manchester Piccadilly to Manchester Airport. The unit also sports BR standard blue and grey livery, applied from the late 1960s.* **Author**

Below: <u>Class AM5/Class 305.</u> *Almost identical in design to the AM4s was the AM5 fleet, originally built for Great Eastern line use and delivered in two batches — 52 three-car sets and 19 four-car units. The units were powered by GEC traction equipment and wired for dual-voltage operation. The sets remained operating in their intended area until the late 1980s when displaced by more modern stock, some sets then going to work in Yorkshire, the Manchester area and even in Scotland. Set No 305507 is illustrated at Stockport on 7 January 1992 painted in Regional Railways livery.* **Author**

Above and Below: <u>Class AM2/Class 302.</u> *112 4-car Class AM2s were built between 1958-61 for use on the LTS 'Tilbury' line. Allocation was between East Ham and Ilford and sets remained in service until the late 1990s. To improve the operation and passenger perception of the sets in the 1980s, 30 were given major refurbishment, which resulted in internal gangways fitted, revised seating and internal layout. After completing passenger work some sets entered departmental use. Above is three-car set No 302996 painted in green and tan livery and used as a depot tractor unit at Ilford, and during the autumn months as a Sandite rail adhesion improvement train. The set is seen at Ilford on 19 May 1989. The illustration below shows set No 302993, also modified as a three-car set and rebuilt by Ilford for Royal Mail letter and parcel traffic on GE lines. This was one of four sets modified with roller shutter doors in 1989-90 and operated until 1996. On 29 July 1992 the unit is seen at Ipswich painted in full Royal Mail livery, waiting to form a mail service to Liverpool Street. Both:* **Author**

Above: Class AM7/Class 307. *A batch of 32 four-car AM7s was built in 1956 for use on the Liverpool Street-Southend (Victoria) route operating at 1,500V DC. The sets were rebuilt for 25kV AC operation in 1960-1961. Refurbishment in the 1980s saw a much improved interior and gangways between vehicles. The fleet remained on Great Eastern tracks until 1990. Four sets were then transferred to Leeds for use on the Leeds–Doncaster route. The fleet was withdrawn in 1993. The majority of driving cars were then rebuilt as Propelling Control Vehicles (PCVs) for Royal Mail use. On 27 July 1990, sets No 307118 and 307120 are seen at Leeds City station.* **Author**

Below: Class AM8/Class 308. *A total of 33 AM8 four-car sets were built to the standard BR EMU design in 1961 for use on Liverpool Street outer-suburban duties. The sets eventually worked on the LTS routes and by 1993 were transferred away, firstly to Bletchley for use on the Birmingham Cross-City line and later to Leeds for the Aire Valley electrification. The fleet was eventually withdrawn in 2001. Painted in West Yorkshire red and cream livery, set No 308152 is seen at Doncaster on 5 April 1995 forming the 15.18 stopping service to Leeds.* **Author**

Above: <u>Class AM9/Class 309.</u> *By far the most handsome of the Great Eastern EMUs were the 23 units of Class AM9 built for use on the Liverpool Street–Clacton/Walton routes in 1962. Originally painted in BR maroon with rounded cab windows, these were the first EMUs designed for 100mph operation. In maroon livery, set No 618 is seen at Clacton.* **Author's collection**

Right: *The 309s were withdrawn between 1994 and 2000 and stored, later being sold for scrap. Two sets were transferred to Railtrack for departmental use as cab-signal development sets for West Coast upgrade work. Renumbered as a Class 960, set No 101 is seen at Old Dalby.* **Author**

Below: *A magnificent line-up of AC power at Ilford depot on 4 June 1970, with units of Classes AM6, AM5, AM2 and AM9 visible.* **Author**

Above and Below: <u>Class AM10/Class 310.</u> *Between 1965 and 1967 a fleet of 50 four-car Class AM10 units were built for the electrification of the London—Birmingham/Manchester/Liverpool routes. These were a novel new design, based on the Mk2 passenger coach and incorporated very pleasing front ends with wrap-around cab front windows. Initially painted in all-over BR rail blue, the sets allocated to Bletchley Depot were soon repainted into standard blue and grey colours. Above, Set No 047 is illustrated soon after delivery. After 1988, with deployment of refurbished Class 317s on LM duties, the AM10 started to be transferred to the LTS route, allocated to East Ham. A small number were also transferred north to operate in the Birmingham area until the full compliment of Class 323s were introduced. From the late 1980s sets were repainted in Network SouthEast colours and a few were repainted into Regional Railway colours. Set No 310049 seen below is at Ilford depot in NSE livery on 30 March 1992.* **Author's collection/Author**

The AC Electrics

Above: Class 312. *To provide additional main-line standard EMUs in the mid-1970s, the Class 310 design was refined with the latest equipment and a batch of Class 312s were built. Originally 26 sets were for Great Northern use, 19 sets for Great Eastern and four for the Birmingham area. Eventually all were allocated to the Great Eastern and then to the LTS line, from where they were withdrawn in 2002. Painted in NSE livery, No 312730 is seen at Ilford on 19 May 1989.* **Author**

Middle: Class 313. *Derived from the 1972-design prototype PEP unit, the Class 313 became the first of the 1970s suburban stock. A fleet of 64 three-car sets was built by BREL York for Great Northern London Division local services. To enable operation to Moorgate which was electrified using the third rail direct current system, these sets were dual AC/DC sets, able to work from 25kV AC overhead or 750V DC third rail. The sets remain the mainstay on suburban services on the GN route, but today a batch are operated by Silverlink Railways on their Euston–Watford and Richmond–Stratford services. As built the sets were outshopped in blue/grey; this later changed to NSE colours and now the Silverlink and FCC livery. Set No 313048 is seen at Hornsey.* **Author**

Right: Class 314. *When new suburban AC units were ordered for Glasgow area use, the same basic 1972-design was followed, with a batch of 16 three-car sets delivered in 1979. The sets were originally painted in BR blue/grey, later in Strathclyde orange and now in carmine and cream of the Strathclyde PTE. Set No 314203 is seen at Milngavie.* **Author**

Above and Below: <u>Class 315.</u> *When replacement stock was sought for the London Liverpool Street to Shenfield suburban route, standard 1972-design stock was stipulated. This time due to passenger numbers a total of 61 four-car sets were ordered, each able to seat 318 passengers. Allocated from delivery in 1980-81 to Ilford, and deployed on their original route right until the present day, the fleet has given outstanding service. The units are now deployed on a wider Great Eastern route remit. Originally painted in blue grey livery, the sets were repainted in mid-1980s NSE colours and more recently in First Great Eastern livery, WAGN purple and now 'one' Railways colours. Above set No 315855 is shown in NSE livery at Ilford on 19 May 1989, while set No 315809 is seen below at Shenfield. A repaint in 1997 saw the application of First Great Eastern colours. Both:* **Author**

Above: Class 316. *In 1990, to test the effects of regenerative braking on three-phase drive packages, three former Class 210 DMU cars and a Class 313 trailer were formed together by the RTC Derby and operated on the Great Eastern route, principally on the Clacton line. Each of the driving cars was fitted with Brush Traction equipment while the '313' car had its equipment repositioned inside the passenger saloon area. The set is seen at Clacton on 5 April 1990.* **Author**

Above Right and Right: Class 317.
Designed originally for the 'Bed-Pan' line from St Pancras to Bedford when it was electrified in 1981-82, this fleet originally consisted of 48 4-car sets, classified 317/1. In 1985-87 a further fleet of 24 Class 317/2s were introduced for Great Northern use. By the end of 1987 the original '317s' were replaced on the Midland route by Class 319s and the '317s' found work on the Euston-Northampton line for a short period before moving to Hornsey for GN work. Further use change came in 1997 when a batch was moved to East Ham for LTS line use. Today the fleet is allocated to Ilford for Great Eastern area use. Major refurbishment has been carried out over the years and some sets used on the Stansted Airport route have a revised body profile on the cab ends. The middle view shows Class 317/1 No 317307 in NSE livery at Hornsey, while the lower view shows 317/2 No 317357 with revised body style at Hornsey on 23 March 1992. Both: **Author**

Above: Class 318. With the 1982 approval for the electrification from Paisley to Ayr came the authorisation for 21 three-car Class 318s, which were to the same basic design as the second phase of the Class 317s. The all-standard-class sets started to emerge from BREL York Works in June 1986, painted in Strathclyde orange. These highly successful sets were refurbished from 2001 and are now painted in the latest Strathclyde carmine and cream livery. Set No 318261 is seen at Glasgow Central on 22 March 1994. **Author**

Above Left and Left: <u>Class 319.</u> Designed for use on the dual-voltage 'Thameslink' route, the Class 319s have been another very successful design, being constructed at York Works. In addition to working Thameslink services for NSE, latterly in the private sector, currently First Capital Connect, the '319s' have also operated for Connex and more recently Southern. The illustration above left shows Class 319/0 No 319009 painted in standard NSE colours, at London Bridge on 26 March 1994 forming a service to Brighton. The bottom view shows set No 319011 passing Clapham Junction forming a Southern service from Victoria to Horsham. This unit displays the more recent Southern green and white livery. Both illustrations of Class 319s show operation on DC, using their third rail power collection shoes. When in this mode of operation, the 25kV AC pantograph on the roof of one of the middle vehicles is stowed out of use. Both: **Author**

Above: <u>Class 320.</u> *By the time the 22-strong order was placed for North Clyde EMUs in 1989, the standard body design was based on the hugely successful Class 321 style. Allocated to Yoker, these orange-liveried units began to appear from June 1990, entering service from the October timetable change. These sets have standard class interiors and are now refurbished, sporting the latest carmine and cream livery. Sets Nos 320321 and 320322 stand in the works yard at BREL York on 28 August 1990.* **Author**

Below: <u>Class 322.</u> *A fleet of five Class 322s was ordered by Network SouthEast for use on the Liverpool Street–Stansted Airport service. These were a modified Class 321 fitted with 2+2 seating and luggage stacks. After displacement on the Stansted route, the sets were hired to First North Western and also operated on the Anglia main line. After much reallocation, all five sets are now refurbished and operate on First ScotRail, principally on the North Berwick route. On the day of its delivery, set No 322481 poses at London King's Cross after forming a delivery special from York. The Stansted Express light grey and green livery was always very pleasing to the eye.* **Author**

This page: <u>Class 321.</u> *If any of the modern AC EMU designs could be described as 'standard' it would surely be the Class 321, one of the most trouble-free and best-performing designs of modern electric unit. Designed for use on the Great Eastern outer-suburban lines, the Euston-Birmingham route and on Doncaster-Leeds local electric services, three batches were built, the 321/3s, for Great Eastern, 321/4s for the Euston route and 321/9s for the Leeds area. The 321/3s and 321/4s were set out for low density first/standard class seating while the Leeds sets were all standard class in high-density style. When built, all except the 321/9s were in NSE colours. The 321/9s were finished in Yorkshire maroon and cream. Over the years some cross allocating has taken place with a handful of 321/4s now allocated to Great Eastern routes. Under privatisation the GE sets were first repainted into First Great Eastern colours and this will soon be giving way to 'one' livery. The Euston line sets were repainted into Silverlink livery of mauve and yellow, but this is to change from late 2007 with franchise changes. The Yorkshire sets are still in maroon, but overhauls from 2006 have seen the 'Northern' franchise being reflected in a new-style livery. Class 321/4 No 321443 is shown above at Crewe, while working a Liverpool–Birmingham service. The middle view shows a short lived 3M advertising livery applied to GE set No 321308 at Manningtree on 25 July 1995. The view left shows 321/9 No 321903 at Wakefield Westgate while working a Doncaster–Leeds service.*
All: **Author**

Right: <u>Class 323.</u> *One of the more problematic of the modern classes was this batch of 43 Class 323 3-car sets introduced for Regional Railways and built by Hunslet-TPL of Leeds. The first set was handed over in 1992, but commissioning and structural problems led to a delay until 1996 before the full fleet entered timetabled service. The units were introduced for use on the Birmingham CrossCity electrification, as well as in the Manchester area, especially on services to and from Manchester Airport. Due to the delays in commissioning a number of sets were stored at MoD sites for many months. Set No 323203 is seen at MoD Long Marston.* **Author**

Below: <u>Class 325.</u> *With hindsight these 16 dual-voltage Royal Mail Class 325 sets should never have been ordered. Introduced in 1995 and funded by Royal Mail, these sets were intended to revolutionise rail postal services. They could operate from 750V DC third rail or 25kV AC overhead and had front-end jumpers allowing coupling to main-line diesel and electric locomotives. Based on Class 319 technology, the sets were built at ABB Derby, each four-car set consisting of four open vans, with a driving cab at the outer ends. Access was by two roller-shutter doors on each side of each coach. Following Royal Mail's decision to pull out of rail operations due to contractual difficulties with operator EWS, the sets were stored. A handful were returned to rail use in 2006, operated by First GBRf on London—Scotland Royal Mail flows. Set No 325005 is seen at ABB Derby.* **Author**

Above: <u>Class 332.</u> *For the electrification of the Paddington-Heathrow Airport line in 1998 a batch of 14 units was ordered from Siemens Transportation; classified as 332, these sets had their bodies built by CAF in Spain and were fitted out in Germany. Originally built as three-car sets, much reformation has been carried out and today half the fleet operates as five-car sets and the remainder as four-car units. Interiors are for first- and standard-class travel with extra space for air travellers' luggage. Sporting grey Hex livery, set No 332007 is seen at Paddington during testing on 18 December 1997.* **Author**

Below: <u>Class 333.</u> *Delivered in 2000 for the Leeds-area electrification project, this fleet of originally three-car (later four-car) Class 333s was structurally the same as the Heathrow Express Class 332s, again built in Spain and Germany. Painted in West Yorkshire PTE maroon livery, originally offset by Northern Spirit branding, the sets are usually referred to as 'Metro Trains' and are all allocated to Leeds Neville Hill. Set No 333010 is seen at Bradford.* **Author**

Right: <u>Class 303.</u> *For the late 1950s electrification of the Glasgow suburban area a fleet of 'Blue Trains', three-car sliding door sets were introduced. A total of 91 sets in various batches was assembled by Scottish firm Pressed Steel. The sets remained in their dedicated area, first painted in Caledonian blue, later BR blue and blue/grey before being painted in Strathclyde orange. In the 1980s, with no replacement sets on the cards, a major refurbishment scheme was launched. The sets remained in traffic until replaced by Class 334s in 2000-02. Set No 303025 is seen at Motherwell on 4 June 1996.* **Author**

Middle: <u>Class 303.</u> *Between 1981 and 1983 13 Scottish Class 303s were transferred to the Manchester area, where they operated until 1991. Painted in Manchester orange and brown livery, set No 303053 is seen at Ilford depot on 19 May 1989, just prior to the set being disposed of by Vic Berry, Leicester.* **Author**

A fleet of 19 Class 311s, almost identical to the Class 303s, was introduced in 1966/7 for South Clyde services, being built by Cravens and remaining in service until 1987-90.

Below: <u>Class 334.</u> *The new generation of Scottish EMU power was introduced from 1999 when a fleet of 40 GEC-Alstom 'Juniper' Class 334 units were launched. Although plagued with major problems, the fleet has now settled down. These three-car sets are finished in carmine and cream. No 334006 is seen at Ayr.* **Author**

Above: <u>Class 350.</u> *The Siemens 'Desiro' product line has become a common sight around the electrified network in recent years with versions in AC, DC and dual voltage being built. The fleet of 30 Class 350s operated jointly by Silverlink and Central Trains and based at Northampton now forms the backbone of stopping services on the Euston—Birmingham corridor and operate through services to Liverpool and Preston. These high-quality four-car sets are gangwayed throughout, allowing 12-car formations to operate. Until franchise changes take effect in late 2007, the sets are finished in grey livery with blue doors. Set No 350112 is seen at Northampton.* **Author**

Middle: <u>Class 360/1.</u> *The first of the AC-powered 'Desiro' sets to enter traffic were 21 sets for Great Eastern (at the time First Great Eastern). These are non-corridor-end sets sporting a full-width driving cab and are used on outer suburban Liverpool Street services. Seating is provided for first and standard class passengers and sets are allocated to Ilford Depot. Sporting its First swirl livery, set No 360115 departs from Colchester on 8 September 2006 forming the 13.08 Liverpool Street to Clacton service.* **Author**

Left: <u>Class 360/2.</u> *To provide stock for a joint First Great Western/BAA stopping service from London Paddington to Heathrow Airport, a batch of five Class 360/2 sets have been introduced. Four of these sets were rebuilt from prototype Class 350 sets originally built with end gangways for type testing, while the fifth unit was built from new. Delivered as four-car sets, passenger growth dictated that an additional trailer was added soon after introduction. This batch of the Desiro family was in keeping with the rest of the design and was built at the Siemens factory in Uerdingen, Germany and tested on the company's test track at Wildenrath, where this view of set No 360203 was taken on 4 November 2004 during a press demonstration run. These five 'Heathrow Connect' units are fitted with Great Western Automatic Train Protection equipment.* **Author**

Above: <u>Class 365.</u> *The norm in recent years has been to design and build modern EMUs for dual-voltage operation, enabling lease owners to have a better chance of hiring their charges at franchise changes. The fleets are usually wired for either AC or DC use and then commissioned with one system operational. Some of the first dual-voltage sets were the 'Networker Express' units built at York for allocation to south and north Thames routes. Set No 365528, a set destined for AC operation is seen at Doncaster on 25 June 1996 during commissioning. These sets were designed for Great Northern outer-suburban use. All are now allocated to Hornsey and have refurbished front ends.* **Author**

Below: <u>Class 357.</u> *The Bombardier 'Electrostar' product range has been offered and supplied in a number of AC, DC and dual voltage designs. The early 'Electrostar' products were for the London Tilbury & Southend route where two batches of Class 357s were deployed. This railway was later branded 'c2c'. These sets encompass the 'standard' ABB/Bombardier cab as used on the diesel 'Turbostar' product range. Painted in full c2c livery, set No 357001 passes Ripple Lane on 17 February 2006 with a service bound for London Fenchurch Street.* **Author**

Above and Left: Class 375 and Class 377. *The Bombardier 'Electrostar' product range of Class 375 and 377 has been built for operators South Eastern and Southern in both DC and dual AC/DC versions formed as three- and four-car sets. All units have full gangway connections which requires a rather clumsy front end layout. Sets operated by South Eastern are classified as '375' and those working for Southern '377'. Different seating styles and interior configurations are incorporated in various builds. The view above shows Class 375/9 No 375908 at Ashford, the 375/9 group of 27 units incorporates a slightly high-density seating layout. The lower view shows Class 377 No 377204, painted in Southern livery, at London Bridge. The Class 377/2 classification covers 15 four-car sets fully operational under either AC or DC power supply and are usually deployed on services on the Brighton-Watford corridor, performing an AC/DC power change between Kensington and North Pole Junction.* Both: **Author**

Above: <u>Class 376.</u> *Although built fully compliant for AC/DC operation, the fleet of 36 five-car Class 376 'Electrostar' Metro units is operated by the South Eastern franchise and at present are only configured for DC operation. These sets' interior is very much like that of a tram, with very basic seating and copious amounts of standing room. Although based on the Class 375 'Electrostar' product these sets incorporate standard sliding doors, no end gangways and no toilet facilities. The sets are allocated to Slade Green and operate on the highest density Kent-London commuter services. Set No 376004 is seen at London Bridge on 4 July 2006.*
Author

Right: <u>Class 395.</u> *The first inroad into the UK traction scene by Hitachi Industries of Japan is this fleet of 29 six-car Class 395 units fitted for dual AC/DC operation, which will be used on the new South Eastern-operated domestic service to operate over the Channel Tunnel Rail Link (High Speed 1) route from St Pancras to destinations in Kent. The sets were constructed in 2006-07 and shipped by sea to Southampton from late Summer 2007. The sets have a very distinctive 'bullet' front end, but if the mock-up is to be followed, a very basic passenger interior; this, however, is likely to be acceptable to passengers as the longest time they will be on-board is just over 60 minutes. The Class 395s will be able to operate from DC third rail power systems as well as CTRL 25kV AC, full TVM430 cab signalling will also be fitted. The view right is of a mock-up produced for passenger user groups and for advertising purposes.*
Author

Above/Below: <u>Class 370 (APT).</u> *The electric-powered Advanced Passenger Train — Pre-production (APT-P) was one of the most remarkable trains ever built in the UK, developed by BR Research in the mid-1970s as a follow-on to the APT-E gas turbine project. A total of six half-trains were built at Derby, each formed of one driving trailer, five trailer passenger vehicles and a power car. Testing of the project commenced in 1978 with diesel power providing traction; from early 1979 electric testing commenced on the West Coast route with the train sets based at Glasgow Shields Road. The train incorporated a tilt feature to allow operation over conventional tracks at increased speeds, but difficulties with this equipment, compounded by lack of finance, eventually saw the project fail, but not before a huge amount of research into high-speed train operation had been gained, much of which was later incorporated into projects such as Virgin Trains' Pendolino. The view above shows a short-formed Class 370 APT set between Penrith and Carlisle in June 1979, while the view below shows a complete 12-car formation, led by set No 370005 at Euston on 8 August 1980 during a test run from London to Carlisle. Both:* **Author**

Above: <u>Class 370 (APT).</u> *The first complete set of APT vehicles, including a driving trailer, trailer standard, trailer brake first and a power car stand in the yard of the Engineering Development Unit, Derby in March 1979. At this time the branding on the powercar read 'InterCity APT' and no frontal branding was applied.* **Author**

Right and Below: <u>Class 390.</u> *Love them or hate them, Virgin Trains' route modernisation of the West Coast Main line between 2000 and 2005 with the introduction of 53 125mph Pendolino train sets has revolutionised rail travel on the West Coast route. The tilting Pendolino train sets, built by Alstom, have distributed power using a 25kV AC supply. The nine-car formation, using a fixed formation layout, was originally designed for 140mph operation using full 'in-cab' automatic cab signalling, but as this has not been authorised the sets remain governed to a top speed of 125mph. Sets include first- and standard-class accommodation in rather cramped conditions due to the restricted 'tilt' loading gauge. On the right is the interior of a standard-class vehicle, while below set No 390010 arrives at Manchester Piccadilly with a service from London Euston on 25 July 2005. Both:* **Author**

Eurostar - Class 373

Design: GEC-Alstom
Number range: 3001-3314
Introduced: 1992-95
Withdrawn: All still active

Without doubt the most impressive trains to operate in the UK are Eurostar's, working between the UK and France/Belgium via The Channel Tunnel. The trains, capable of multi-voltage operation, were ordered in 1989, but prior to that, discussions between the three main railway administrations, BR (UK), SNCF (France) and SNCB (Belgium) had taken place to establish the type of train needed.

The most desirable option was to use French TGV trains, while the UK favoured a more conventional loco-hauled consist. Eventually the TGV-style option was followed and through European Passenger Services (EPS), a wholly-owned subsidiary of the BRB, trains were ordered from Alstom.

Huge problems existed in developing a Channel Tunnel train, capable of working over the rail systems of three countries, as well as through the Channel Tunnel; all had specific operating and rule structures and all were loath to change any principles. The main area of change was the most obvious, that of loading gauge, on the BR network, as more restricted space was available between the train and structures compared to mainland Europe, which used the UIC or Berne gauge.

Eventually a design consortium of De Dietrich, Ateliers de Construction Electrique de Charleroi (ACEC Transport), BN Division de Bombardier Eurorail, GEC-Alsthom Transportation, Metro-Cammell and Brush. The leading voice was GEC Alsthom.

Mechanically, the design followed the French TGV, but many changes were needed for UK operation, including the physical size. To maximise throughput of trains through the Channel Tunnel, long formations of 20 coaches were specified. The axle-load had to be kept down to the TGV standard of 17 tonnes, as in France and Belgium the sets would operate over conventional TGV lines. On power cars, traction motors had to be body-mounted rather than bogie-mounted, which assisted in reducing track wear. An articulated design was eventually accepted, which permitted lower-slung vehicles.

The contract for Eurostar trains was signed in December 1989, for 30 20-vehicle sets. Subsequently a follow-on order was placed, giving a fleet of 31. This number was increased following agreement for 'north of London' operation and a further seven shorter (16-car) trains were ordered.

Ownership of Eurostars, known in the UK as Class 373, is complex; the original European Passenger Services, now Eurostar UK owns 18 sets, including the seven regional trains, SNCF 16 sets and SNCB four sets. Construction of the trains was divided between the participating countries, split by percentage 40:40:20 (France/England/Belgium).

The 31 20-car trains are each formed of two identical half-train 10-coach formations, with a driving power car and nine passenger cars, the one coupled to the power car also having traction equipment. A full 20-vehicle Eurostar seats 210 first and 584 standard class passengers, giving a total of 794 seats per train.

The Regional sets, formed of 16 vehicles - two driving and 14 saloons gave seating for 578 (114 first and 464 standard class).

The Eurostar sets are without doubt the most complex trains in the world. By virtue of the routes operated, they have to work from three different power supplies including both AC and DC obtained from both the third rail and overhead collection systems, as well as operating over four different railway administrations. The change-over between the different power supplies and operating modes is carried out while on the move, with the train running into 'dead' or neutral sections. The action to change power is effected manually by the driver.

At an early stage in the project it was agreed that the Eurostar sets would be built at various plants in Europe and then 'formed up' as full train consists at either Belfort in France or Washwood Heath in Birmingham.

The first Eurostar was assembled at Belfort in 1992. Identified originally as PS1, it was formed of just seven coaches and two power cars, it was delivered for test running in January 1993. Its first powered runs were between Strasbourg and Mulhouse. By June 1993 the set was transferred to the UK for DC tests, arriving on 20 June 1993.

In May 1993, a second pre-service set, PS2 — a full 20-car train — was delivered for testing. After shakedown trials from Le Landy (Paris), the set started high-speed running on the Paris–Lille line in July, when, for the first time a Eurostar reached its maximum passenger operating speed of 300km/h (186mph).

The first UK-built train, UK1, actually formed of Belgian half-sets Nos 3101/02, was delivered from Washwood Heath to North Pole Depot in West London on 31 October 1993.

Eurostar passenger trains commenced operation from Waterloo International to Paris and Brussels in autumn 1994, with, at first, two trains per day to each destination. Development of the Eurostar operation has been such that a UK high speed line between the Channel Tunnel and London was needed; this progressively opened in two sections, the route between Ebbsfleet and the Channel Tunnel in 2004 and that between London St Pancras (the new London terminal) and mid-Kent from November 2007. At the same time, new purpose-built maintenance facilities for the entire Eurostar fleet were built at Stratford in East London, the original North Pole site in West London and the Waterloo International terminal being mothballed.

Regrettably the proposed Regional or North of London service was never launched, due to far lower than expected patronage and serious technical issues.

After the Regional service was abandoned, the short sets were stored. In 2000 three entered a hire contract with GNER to supplement services at first on the King's Cross–York and then the King's Cross–Leeds corridors. This contract came to an end in 2005.

When introduced the Eurostar sets were finished in a distinctive white and blue livery with full yellow ends. The first livery change came in 1999 when full train length advertising liveries were introduced on a small number of sets. The sets operated by GNER were also reliveried into full GNER dark blue.

One spare power car, No 3999, was built, which can be used within any set and is usually, when not in use, kept at the North Pole depot.

After introduction and lower than expected passenger figures on the Cross-Channel route, a small number of French-owned sets were modified for French domestic-only use, these had the third rail DC power collection shoes removed and a livery modification made, including the removal of the yellow front ends.

Further modifications were made to some Cross-Channel sets to allow operation into 1,500V DC areas in Southern France and in the French Alps, allowing a restricted through international service from the UK to popular holiday destinations and ski resorts.

Above: *From route opening in 1994 until November 2007, the Eurostar stock used 750V DC third rail power collection in the UK. This was first reduced in 2005 by the opening of the first section of the Channel Tunnel Rail Link, which saw overhead electrification through Kent, including Ashford International Station. On 23 June 2006, Belgian-owned set No 373105 stops at Ashford International using AC power, forming the 08.39 Waterloo International–Brussels service.* **Author**

Left: *All the Eurostar body shells were assembled in Belfort, France, at the principal GEC-Alstom erection site. However, to allow the UK an equal part of the Anglo-French project, around half the build was then shipped to the UK for fitting out and testing. The power car and associated motor car for set No 373014 (a UK set) are seen in the final test area at GEC-Alstom, Washwood Heath, Birmingham on 25 March 1994.* **Author**

Below: *Operating at 300kmh (186mph), over the TGV Nord route near Beaumont, French-owned sets Nos. 373206/205 form the 16.23 Waterloo International–Paris Nord service on 11 July 1996. A major refurbishment project on Eurostar train interiors was carried out from 2004 to bring the passenger environment into line with French domestic TGV stock.* **Author**

Above: *Until the construction of phase one of the CTRL, Eurostar services traversed UK domestic tracks through Kent. One unusual location was Willesborough, south of Ashford, where a manual level crossing existed. There could be but few locations where the world's fastest train could be found passing a manual crossing! On 7 July 1994, set No 373008 passes Willesborough with the 14.48 Paris Nord–Waterloo service.* **Author**

Below: *Sets No 373203/204/225-228 have been removed from Eurostar ownership and transferred to the domestic SNCF TGV fleet for operating services either on the Paris–Lille or South of France routes. On 16 April 2002, sets Nos. 373203/204 stop at Avignon forming the 09.01 Nice–Bruxelles Midi service. These six half-train sets have had all UK DC power equipment and UK AWS removed. The original North London sets have now joined the domestic French fleet operating on the Brussels/Lille-Paris route.* **Author**

Above: *To provide maintenance facilities for the Eurostar train fleet upon service introduction, depots were built in France, Belgium and the UK. The UK facility was at North Pole, in West London, where a split shed for service and heavy maintenance was provided. Protruding from the London end of the service shed, set No 373101 is seen on 9 December 1993. The depot was principally equipped for 25kV AC operation, with short third-rail DC sections.* **Author**

Below: *Sporting GNER dark blue livery, one of three North of London sets hired to GNER, No 3304, is seen approaching London King's Cross on a 'White Rose' service from York. The hire of these sets finished in 2005 and Eurostar are now to deploy the sets on domestic French duties, meaning that they are unlikely to be seen back in the UK after mid-2007.* **Author**

Eurotunnel 'Shuttle'

Above: *The Eurotunnel Tri-Bo locomotives are the only three-bogie locomotives to operate in the UK; the method of mounting was dictated by very tight curvature within the 'loops' at both Cheriton in the UK and Coquelles in France. Although built by Brush Traction in Loughborough, traction equipment was supplied by ABB. No 9025 is illustrated when new fitted with 5,760kW equipment. This locomotive has now been refurbished and fitted with 7,000kW traction equipment and reclassified as a Class 9/8 renumbered 9825.* **Author**

Prior to the opening of the Channel Tunnel, operator Eurotunnel placed with Brush Traction an order for 38 single-ended locomotives in the late 1980s, during the early phase of tunnel construction work. The locomotives were, and are still unique, in the UK, being mounted on three two-axle bogies, thus giving a Bo-Bo-Bo (or Tri-Bo) configuration permitting operation around very tight curves within the Eurotunnel terminal network.

The Shuttle locomotives are built to a non-standard gauge envelope and are not allowed to operate outside the Eurotunnel system, working on a 'loop' between Cheriton (Folkestone) in the UK and Coquelles (Calais) in France.

The locomotive bodies were fabricated at Qualter Hall Engineering, Barnsley and fitted out at Brush Traction. To meet stringent Channel Tunnel operating requirements, the locomotives are virtually two electric locomotives in one body, ensuring that only the most serious failures can stop a train from proceeding.

Numbered in a Eurotunnel 9xxx series, the original fleet of 38 locomotives was delivered to Coquelles. Soon after the Channel Tunnel opened, growth was encouraging and a follow-on order was placed, but this batch only had driving controls at the leading end (the original order had a remote driver's cab at the slab end). Other modifications rendered this batch as a separate sub-class and were thus numbered in the 91xx series.

A further batch of locomotives was ordered in late 1999 with a 7MW output. These were to the same basic body style, and numbered in the 97xx series, being used only for freight shuttle haulage.

All locomotives were finished in Eurotunnel livery, with the 90xx machines carrying a green and blue band at cantrail height. This is now being replaced by a Eurotunnel livery, developed after the original trading title of 'Le Shuttle' was dropped. Soon after delivery all 90xx locomotives were all given names.

In normal operating, a Tri-Bo 'shuttle' locomotive is coupled at each end of a train, with both locos working under the control of the leading driver. If a problem is encountered *en route*, the on-board train captain uses the cab in the rear locomotive and splits the train, allowing two separate portions to be removed from the tunnel.

Two types of train are operated by 'Shuttle' locomotives; Freight Shuttles, which transport freight road trucks, and Tourist Shuttles, which transport motor cars, coaches and bicycles.

All locomotives are equipped to operate only from the Eurotunnel overhead power system at 25kV AC and are based at purpose-built accommodation at the Coquelles terminal; their space envelope prevents them from operating outside the Shuttle system.

One locomotive has been withdrawn, No 9030, which was the rear locomotive involved in the Channel Tunnel fire; new locomotive No 9040 was built as a replacement.

A major refurbishment programme commenced in 2004, seeing all the original 90xx locomotives pass through Brush Traction for significant upgrading; on completion locomotives are renumbered into the 98xx series, retaining their last two digits of the original number.

Above: *Emerging from the Channel Tunnel in France, Shuttle locomotive No 9030, which was later destroyed in the Channel Tunnel fire on 18 November 1996, leads the 11.53 Cheriton to Coquelles tourist service into the French daylight on 17 November 1994.* **Author**

Right: *Photography of the Shuttle trains is very difficult, especially now that vegetation has grown up around the construction sites and extra fences have been erected due to increased security. Before the trees grew up at Cheriton, Kent, Shuttle locomotive No 9016 arrives with a full-length tourist shuttle from Coquelles on 13 October 1995. The four tracks on the left of the train are the through lines used by Eurostar and freight services.* **Author**

Following Page: *On 3 July 1994, 9/0 Shuttle locomotive No 9012 brings up the rear of an arriving Shuttle at the Cheriton terminal in Kent. On this day freight loadings must have been rather low as empty vehicles are seen on the rear of the train. At this point, the train is turning around the loop to reach the offloading platform and passing below the main terminal and vehicle holding area.* **Author**